I0838882

SOCIOLOGY FOR CONSERVATIVES

An American Conservative Social Theory
2021

Charles Moscowitz

Introduction

First, a bit about myself…

Majoring in sociology at Bunker Hill Community College in Boston, Massachusetts, I am a first-time college student who is nearing retirement age. In this regard, I offer the viewpoint of a boomer who came of age in the sixties and seventies. As a result of not having gone to college in my youth, I did not develop the styles and modes of thinking that typify what has been euphemistically referred to as the eastern seaboard liberal establishment. I left home after high school, 1975, to pursue a career in music which did not materialize. I worked at various unskilled jobs and started my own business in the mid-eighties. I married in 1990 and our daughter was born in 1998. My business became successful in the nineties and then went belly up in 2006 which left me feeling emotionally bereft.

My work included spending a good deal of time in the car where I fell in love with talk radio. I filed my first tax return as a self-employed businessman in 1986. These experiences, along with a growing belief in God, led me away from the liberalism that I had always known. I became conservative and yet, paradoxically, I retained elements of the sixties counter-culture that questions authority. One motto that might be sited as best describing the mission of Sociology, coined by Sociologist Peter Berger is: *Things are not what they seem to be.*

I was influenced toward conservatism by radio talk show hosts including Jerry Williams, David Brudnoy, Gene Burns, and later Rush Limbaugh, Howie Carr and Michael Savage. I began hosting my own radio talk show at WMFO- Tufts in 1996 and I would go on to host radio shows in small markets in Greater Boston where I sold air time and interviewed academics, authors and media figures. My resulting deep dive into politics led me into writing blogs, articles and eventually books. In 2004, I ran for Congress in Massachusetts against Rep. Barney Frank in a race that included an interesting and contentious clash of ideas and several debates with the notorious congressman. Today, besides attending Bunker Hill Community College, authoring books and driving Uber, I host an interview program on YouTube and subscribing podcast platforms. I am an ardent supporter of former President Donald Trump and I listen regularly to Jeff Kuhner on WRKO and to various podcasts including Stephen K. Bannon's War Room Pandemic.

I enter into my latter years of life with a sense of gratitude and with a lot of regrets for a life filled with successes and failures, pride and shame, goodness and sin. As I reflect on my life, I feel grateful for the privilege of having been born and raised in this great American nation which I view as exceptional, a civilization that I view as to be the manifestation of the best principles and ideals of mankind. The Sociological Imagination, as described by sociologist C. Wright Mills, challenges us to examine our personal lives and personal histories in the broad context of a study of the society in which we live and its historical antecedents. Sociology, while challenging us to examine the positive as well as the negative elements of our society and of society in general, includes a dynamic element as sociology has been and can be utilized as a force for change.

A sociological imagination has led many capable and accomplished social scientists in the direction of developing important and influential schools of thought and their contributions have led to social change in terms of how we live, how we think, how we perceive our lives, how our societies are crafted and how our societies function. In this short treatise, I shall humbly present an alternative Conservative theory of Sociology, a theory that I hope might contribute in some way toward the development of deeper thinking and research on the part of those who are more qualified than me. I should note, and I do not believe that I am going too far out on a limb by noting this, that Sociology, from its inception, has been and remains a primary incubator and a repository of left leaning and leftist ideas and, as such, has often served as a tool for left-leaning and leftist agendas.

I describe my sociological theory as one that is deviant when viewed in the broad context of sociological work. A basic axiom of Sociology is that deviance from the norm serves as a counterpoint that could be utilized as a means to mold and to shape normative social theorizing and, as such, deviant theory might affect positive change both in society and in individual life. The core contention of my conservative social theory is that conservativism naturally lends itself to sociological theory because conservatism, as a social idea, is most reflective of the better nature of the individual and society. Conservativism is a repository of practical ideas and institutions that work which is why I contend that conservatism offers the most practical and effective lens by which we might view society. Conservatism involves a quest toward the identification of that which is real and that which is true. For this reason, my paradoxical contention is that conservatism is the most applicable foundation upon which positive social change can be effected.

Sociology for Conservatives

Conservatism lends itself to Sociology as it represents the best expression of that which is real and that which is natural and normal to human nature. In this sense, conservatism is not an ideology, per se, but conservatism is an anti-ideology. Conservatism seeks to understand the positive and moral elements of human nature while at the same time identifying negative and immoral tendencies. Conservativism supports institutions and ideas that advance the positive and moral elements of life and society while seeking to reform and modernize those same ideas and institutions in areas in which they are flawed. Conservatism is a study of reality, a study of that which is and is not. Conservatism, deriving from this foundation, offers the best path forward for society and individual life, which is why, in the literal sense, conservatism is progressive.

I differentiate between conservative social theory, conservative political theory and politics. While conservative social theory is a study of that which is true, that which is right and that which is best for a healthy life, while conservatism promotes society established on foundations of truth, conservative politics can involve compromise while adhering to core values as well as deviation and error. One example of how this differentiation becomes manifest regards the question of abortion. Conservative social theory acknowledges that to abort or destroy a human fetus is an act of murder. The fetus is alive before the abortion and the fetus is dead after the abortion which means that the fetus was deliberately killed as a result of an abortion. This is an irrefutable fact.

Yet conservative politics, while animated and guided by the aforementioned fact and by its obvious moral implications, nevertheless might consider extenuating circumstances when advocating public policy regarding abortion such as the life, the interests, and the ultimate choice of the individual pregnant mother. While politics is an art and science of difficult compromise, conservative politics nevertheless remains guided by moral principles and by truth. It should be noted that questions such as abortion, the death penalty, euthanasia, suicide, wars of aggression are moral questions that transcend politics because they address the most fundamental questions that any and all societies grapple with which is the meaning and value of human life. Conservative social theory always errs on the side of life in this regard.

Another example of the differentiation between social and political theory is the question of same-sex marriage. Conservative social theory recognizes the definition of marriage as an event where two opposite elements merge together to create a new element. The male and the female are two distinct and different biological human beings with two distinct and different anatomies. Science indicates that these two separate anatomies were created to come together, ultimately, as a means to procreate and to potentially create a new life. The natural dialectic of two opposites coming together to create a new synthesis is observable in nature as in the animal kingdom. This is the literal definition of marriage.

Yet conservative politics, in a process of assimilating societal realities, might support same-sex civil unions as these institutions have proven to be a sound foundation for a stable relationship and family. Indeed, these unions potentially possess the conservative element of restraining a tendency toward promiscuity that was previously more common to the gay male, a tendency that was problematic in terms of health risks and moral and social concerns. While conservative political theory need not condone same-sex marriage, conservative politics involves a process by which at times conflicting interests might find a means to co-exist in the interest of maintaining individual dignity as well as in the interest of societal cohesion and comity.

The first principle of conservative social theory is a singular belief in one God as the creator of the universe, as the giver of the laws of nature and as the creator of the moral and ethical laws that govern mankind. Having said this, an atheist may be a conservative if they believe in a semantic approximation to a divine source of creation and truth, an outside and immutable force as the objective source of morality and truth. Either way, conservativism holds that both concrete and abstract axioms of existence, of life, of society, and indeed of reality itself exists as an objective and immutable truth, one that resides outside the subjective and imperfect manipulative powers and perceptions of fallible human beings.

Conservatives believe in an objective immutable moral and ethical code based upon identifiable rational truth as derived from a natural or supernatural source. Conservatives hold mankind responsible for identifying and studying that code and then harnessing its innate power in the direction of the progressive development of individual life and social and civic norms. The individual conservative judges and measures his or her own life, and that of others, in contrast to this code as an objective standard of truth. The conservative then makes life decisions based upon those judgements. Conservatives believe that progress is built upon the process of identifying truths and that the knowledge of these truths becomes the foundation upon which individual and social progress is based.

Conservatives believe that God created every human being in his image and, as such, that every single life is of equal value. This principle, which is explicit to the biblical narrative of Genesis, and which finds an eloquent secular expression in the American Declaration of Independence, recognizes that all men are created equal. The American declaration recognized that all rights come from *the creator*. This principle provides the foundation of the American political and social philosophy. Conservatives believe in a concept by which God, or as Thomas Jefferson expressed in secular terms *nature and nature's God*, is the great sovereign of the universe, the creator and the grantor of all rights. God grants a limited temporary degree of sovereignty to the imperfect individual who establishes governments and institutions as means to preserve, protect and defend those God given rights.

The Rev. Dr. Martin Luther King Jr., paraphrasing the 19th century American Unitarian minister Theodore Parker, stated *The arc of the universe is long, but it bends toward justice.* The conservative understanding of a bend toward justice involves the collective acceptance and rejection of ideas and institutions that are either beneficial or detrimental to God-given rights. Since the beginning of time mankind has become more cognizant of ideas and institutions that are detrimental to the interests of the individual and society. With growing awareness of a moral code, mankind has universally rejected such practices as slavery, human sacrifice and cannibalism along with such relationships as those that involving incest and bestiality. Mankind discovered that those institutions were anathema to the well-being, safety, integrity and dignity of the individual man and woman created in the image of God.

America looks to the Bible as the font of moral and ethical law. This is not to suggest that other societies do not also maintain valid functioning moral and ethical codes. This is simply an acknowledgment that the Hebrew Bible happens to serve as the foundation of Western and American religious and secular society. Our civilization was founded upon universal biblical themes as opposed to those biblical themes that might be more applicable to specific religious practice. Those universal themes include prohibitions against murder, rape, and theft. Other more abstract universal themes address the regulation of family, business, property, trade, labor, money, rules of engagement in war, diplomacy between nations and proper forms of government.

Residing at the core of conservatism is the recognition that human beings, who are images of God, are not perfect and, as such, the societies that human beings create are also not and will never be perfect. This is what I mean when I assert that conservatism is natural and, as such, that conservatism is non-ideological. Conservatism examines that which is real and that which is true. Utopianism and perfectibility are not possible as those ideologies are based upon principles that are not real. Indeed, utopian movements such as Communism, Nazism and more recently a radicalized form of Islam and Transhumanism, have caused regression and tragedy in our lives and in our societies because those false ideas inevitably must utilize the force of arms in their attempt to make real something that is not real and will never become real.

The conservative observes that individual and social improvement emanates out of self-interest, free will, love, competition, free association, and by the good works and imagination of individuals and groups. Voluntary social relations between individuals and social comity within society is normal and natural and does not require external force. As human beings, we seek social relations for complex reasons both professional and personal. We seek, by nature, to develop an informal team of people to help us live our lives and accomplish our goals. We are, as such, social animals by nature. Helping our neighbor is a natural part of our being alive and the recognition and promotion of this aspect of our nature is what makes America the most socially conscious and charitable society in history. An example of a private institution that has done more social good than any in history, running hospitals, homes for the elderly, homeless shelters, is the Roman Catholic Church.

The system of competition and self-regulation is based upon the natural principle of individual self-interest as referenced by Scottish moralist and social theorist Adam Smith in his seminal work *Wealth of Nations*, published in 1776. In this great book, a touchstone of modern conservative social theory, Adam Smith referred to the *invisible hand* of the market. The concept of the invisible hand, along with the tempering authority granted to constitutional government as a counterpoint, along with the teaching of moral standards offered by western Christian religion, along with the principle of balance of power, constitutes the primary ideas and institutions of a conservative political and social governing philosophy.

In a conservative social context, the invisible hand, the guiding principle of libertarian theorists, moguls and oligarchs is reined in by conservative moral standards. The invisible hand is reined in by elected governments operating within the structures of subsidiarity and the rule of law as codified by constitutions. The canard of unbridled capitalism, by which anything goes in the name of private ownership, is as false and is as un-natural a concept as communism. Unbridled capitalism, by which the rich hold ruling authority and the minority are unprotected, will eventually devolve into anarchy, fractured forms of localized feudalism, or a trend toward unaccountable international governance. While conservatism encourages the creation and accumulation of wealth, conservatism simultaneously insists upon government and religious safeguards as means to contain the power of wealth and to protect the natural rights of the sovereign individual. Indeed, conservatives view the purpose of government as a vehicle that is created to protect the individual from rapacious capitalism and from foreign invasion among other functions.

The invisible hand functions within the paradigm of a natural system of checks and balances between individuals, business and government. This invisible hand is manifested by the natural moderation of production, wages, prices, and by the supply of goods and services. The invisible hand, on the social level, has the effect of moderating personal excess as honesty and reputation become abstract commodities. The market self-regulates due to the forces of competition, self-interest and by external laws that modify excess. The invisible hand works like a football game where the rules are set, the goal posts are established, and then each man for himself.

The American Constitution reflects this natural principle of checks and balances. In the formal sense, the Federal Government is divided into three branches, each with its own function and each checking and balancing the excess of the other two. This system is replicated on the state and on the local level with national, state and local governments checking and balancing each other. The Bill of Rights balances government with the recognition that the source of power is the citizen under God. These principles were codified into laws including the second, ninth and tenth amendments to the Constitution.

The engine driving the American system of checks and balances, and the operating principle of conservatism, is that the individual is an imperfect being susceptible to error and sin. The conservative understands that the only hope for humanity to mitigate and reduce the intoxicating attraction to sin on a societal level is to diffuse power by means of its relegation and division into numerous and separate silos, each with its own assigned responsibilities, each competing with the other. In our imperfect world, our only hope for achieving degrees of individual freedom and preserving and advancing the civilizational accomplishments that have emanated from individual freedom is by keeping societies that limit and divide power by pitting one entity of power against the other.

Conservatives are nationalists because conservatives understand that the sovereign nation-state is the best expression of that which is natural to the interests of the human being. We establish and organize nations as a means to manage aspects of our lives that are too vast and complex for us to manage on our own or to manage as part of smaller and more specifically defined organizations. The conservative conception of the proper role of the nation-state is that sovereign states are established as means to preserve, protect and defend the God-given natural rights of its citizens. The nation-state as we know it today is a modern social development, one that is progressive and one that is democratic in the real sense because the sovereign nation-state, as an institution, promotes conservative values.

There is a clear difference between the conservative conception of nationalism, which constitutes a dynamic and a genuinely progressive development in human history and politics, and the leftist conception of nationalism which is a corruption of the concept. The conservative conception is that the nation-state derives its powers and its responsibilities from the consent of the governed. The great sovereign, God, grants limited sovereignty to the individual who then establishes limited government as a means to protect that limited sovereignty. The American understanding of the nation-state, and the American philosophy of nationalism, holds that governing powers are checked and are balanced by a written constitution.

Many Americans inherently do not trust government for the same reason that we do not trust powerful corporations or powerful and influential individuals. We seek to preserve the maximum control over our own lives and, as such, we instinctively understand, as British Lord Acton famously noted: *Power corrupts, and absolute power corrupts absolutely.* Government, in the conservative view, holds a limited grant of sovereignty over the individual who, in turn, delegates limited governing authority first to local municipalities, then to the State, and finally to the Federal Government. Each government assumes less powers as it grows in size and distance from the citizen. For example, the conservative conception of government views the highest law-enforcement authority to be the local elected sheriff and the highest authority over public education to be the local elected school board.

Conservatives view the role of the American Federal Government to be a vehicle that regulates issues that affect the national interest such as the regulation of currency, national defense, immigration, diplomacy with foreign nations, international trade policy, and other responsibilities specifically listed in the US Constitution. Conservatives support the promotion of a national ethos, a national language, a loosely defined national culture, a sense of pride and a sense of cohesiveness in a society that has been blessed and has benefited from shared experience and a shared national history. Indeed, the glory of American life, besides the incredible accomplishments of individual Americans living in the milieu of the freedom that was established by the American Revolution, is that we are not a utopia, that we do not seek utopia. As such, we are more willing to learn from and reckon with historic and present mistakes and sins both as individuals and as a people. This contrasts starkly as a historic phenomenon when America is compared to authoritarian systems where individuals and societies tend to lack such confidence and critical self-awareness.

The modern left, in contrast, resurrected the ancient and hoary principle of rule by the god-king. They did this with updated and scientific sounding lingo and garb as they embraced an element of the mid-19th Century European enlightenment concept of the atheistic super-state. They embraced a hyper-nationalistic concept of state control over all aspects of the life of the citizen. Indeed, the original dictionary definition of Socialism, the modern pseudo-scientific governing principle that first reared its head during the French Reign of Terror, is public ownership of the mode of production, of communication, and of the distribution of goods and services. The left advocates for a vague, mystical, utopian definition of the *public* which would assume the governing mantle at some future era, at a time when mankind has achieved the ultimate social goal which would be one world Communism. This social condition would occur when the peoples of the world would become de-facto equal and institutions that foster inequality such as family, property and national borders would have *withered away*, as Marx described it. The underlying philosophy, embraced subconsciously, involves the belief that mankind should be transformed into one gigantic beehive, one that would be in tune with nature and without individual consciousness which would be replaced with a mega-collective fusion into one massive international brain.

Until that great and glorious future arrives, a time when society has evolved to the point of cosmic enlightenment, the hyper-nationalist state run by a clique of enlightened oligarchs acting in the capacity of righteous caretakers and surrogates, would continue to control a nanny superstate serving as a temporary but essential vehicle for transformation and change. Meanwhile, the ruling oligarchs trudge along in the vineyards of the proletariat, sacrificing time and effort for the common good. We should all bow down low and be grateful as they bestow upon the rest of us peons their enlightened services. Thus, they feel perfectly entitled to replace God in heaven with themselves as they clandestinely exercise fiat power over those of us who they view as part of a basket of deplorables.

Decline of the American Family

The general hypothesis regarding the American family is that the conventional American family, consisting of a man and a woman who are married in a committed monogamous relationship with children is in decline. While the traditional family institution, which has constituted the accepted western cultural ideal, may be in decline when viewed in the context of sheer empirical data, I would suggest an alternative hypothesis. I contend that the traditional family, when viewed in a broader context, is not at all in decline but, rather, that the traditional family remains as a thriving institution that remains at the dynamic epicenter of American life and, indeed, at the center of all societies across the globe today. Ironically, my view in this regard is now considered to be the deviant hypothesis as opposed to the norm.

The traditional American family has undergone a conscious and deliberate cultural onslaught, one that accelerated in the 1960's. I contend that the locus of this onslaught involves machinations by what has been loosely described as elements of the eastern seaboard liberal establishment. This establishment, expressing its intentions and its viewpoints through various tools in the popular culture, the media and in the social sciences, has promoted an anti-traditional family view over several decades starting in the 1950's. The traditional family has nevertheless survived and remains intact in spite of the onslaught and the erosion in numbers. This survival is due to its structure which is organic, sovereign and enduring, a structure that has preserved this optimal social institution. The traditional family as we know it today evolved over millennia and has a history that goes back to biblical times and to the times of ancient Rome.

The modern agenda to deconstruct the traditional family could be attributed to the influence of three 19th century social thinkers, Charles Darwin, Karl Marx and Sigmund Freud. Charles Darwin's theory of evolution, putting aside its scientific claims which could be debated in a scientific context, had the philosophical effect of removing the individual human being from the biblical conception that men and women were created in the image of God. Charles Darwin's theory replaced this conception, one which honored every human life as holding a unique spiritual and physical element, with the idea that human beings are an evolved species of enlightened and advanced animals. As such, and as the logical inference of Darwin's scientific theory would hold, collective groups of people were to be viewed as more or as less evolved than other collective groups of people.

Darwin's idea fit hand in glove with an emerging elitist mid-19th century establishment view which went to great lengths to codify his ideas as constituting hard science to be henceforth viewed as an article of faith beyond question. While Darwin clearly viewed his theory from a racist standpoint, thus giving birth to the eugenics movement which was a scientized and modernized form of racism, the overall effect of Darwin's social theory was the cheapening of human life as the survival of the fittest became, as would be expressed by eugenic social thinker Margaret Sanger, a natural means to reduce *dysgenic races* and *useless eaters*.

Karl Marx sought to dedicate his magnum opus, *Capital,* to Charles Darwin who was his contemporary, a dedication that Darwin refused to accept. Marx applied Darwin's biological theory to his own social theory by presenting stages of social as opposed to stages of biological evolution. Marx claimed that his theory of social evolution would advance human society toward a utopian vision of a one world Communist ant colony where institutions such as the traditional family would be done away with, or *made impossible*, as Marx noted in his pamphlet *On the Jewish Question*. Marx social theory suggests a mechanism by which adults are assigned work and professions based upon a perception of their skill and what was needed by the State, in a manner similar to that which was described by ancient Greek philosopher Plato in his book *The Republic*, where children would be raised collectively by appointed experts.

Marx viewed the traditional family as a form of *false consciousness*, an institution that he claimed contributed to inequality and exploitation. Sigmund Freud viewed the traditional family as a form of repression that should be replaced by what he called *polymorphous perversity* by which sexuality would be stripped of prejudices such as love, commitment, sacredness as Freud considered these institutions and ideas as fetishes and forms of emotional bondage and repression. The ideal expression of sexuality, for Sigmund Freud, was anything goes, at any time, with any person or combination of people. Traditional sexual mores, for Freud, who according to many historians was having an adulterous affair with his wife's sister while she was living under the same roof with him and his wife and family, constituted a form of repression wrought by feelings of guilt which Freud viewed as unnatural and psychotic.

American culture was introduced to the deconstruction of the traditional family by social scientists associated with the Frankfurt School of Social Research at Columbia University in the 1950's. This school, which patented critical theory, promoted sexual libertinism as a virtue and as a means to undermine American individualism and capitalism. One of the main exponents of critical theory, German Sociologist Herbert Marcuse, is also viewed as one of the founders of the sexual revolution of the 1960's. Another leader in this regard was Alfred Kinsey, the Rockefeller funded author of *Sexual Behavior and the Human Male*, 1948 and *Sexual Behavior of the Human Female*, 1953. Kinsey, an utterly depraved individual who was marketed by the establishment as a middle of the road bow-tied father figure, conducted dubious and unethical studies which were promoted by the liberal establishment to weaken traditional culture and law.

Structural Functionalism, as patented by early 20th Century French Sociologist Emile Durkheim, holds that there is an organic aspect to most social norms and institutions and that, as such, proper social change should constitute a refinement and improvement of those natural institutions. Functionalism is no longer the main social theory of Sociology today. According to its detractors, functionalism reflects a false paradigm of the happy family as portrayed by the 1950's era sitcom Leave it to Beaver. While functionalism promotes social change within existing social institutions as a means toward reform and improvement, in extreme cases Functionalism advocates that institutions that prove to be deleterious to societal advancement and that are harmful to individuals should be discarded. Such institutions that have been discarded historically include slavery, human sacrifice, cannibalism, and ideas that have proven to be regressive such as racism, collectivism and totalitarianism.

I argue that the social theorists who disregard functionalism are those same thinkers who tend to reject the importance and the dynamic role of the traditional family in society. Functionalism promotes change within the traditional family without throwing the baby out with the bath water. The functionalist would, as an example, seek to re-evaluate the role of the breadwinner as necessarily male, the role of the homemaker as necessarily female, and the functionalist might re-evaluate the role of children in the family or the role of extended family.

Conflict Theory, derived from Marxism, is a social dialectical construct that divides select institutions into two opposing camps. Conflict theory pits each camp against the other in order to create a new synthesis, one that would emerge out of the conflict that might have been either instigated or exacerbated by the theorists themselves or those whom they have influenced. Conflict Theory is based upon the basic conspiracy theory discovered at the core of Marxist thought which holds that half of society, the proletariat, is exploited by the other half of society holding the dominant power, the bourgeoisie. The solution to social problems, for the conflict theorist, is to promote the destruction of both sides as both sides of the conflict are considered beyond redemption. At the end of the conflict, with both sides either altered beyond recognition or destroyed, the critical theorist divides the new synthesis and once again promotes a new dialectical conflict that would emanate out of the new synthesis. Marx described life in the utopia that would emerge out of the last and final apocalyptic worldwide conflict, the emergence of a magical futuristic world, with the slogan *from each according to his ability, to each according to his need.*

Modern feminism was developed by social theorists as an offshoot of conflict theory. This was also the case regarding Critical Legal Theory and Critical Race Theory. While certain aspects of these social theories were cooked up in the proverbial sociological laboratory that was the Frankfurt School of Social Research at Columbia University, nevertheless, like any social theory with staying power these theories derive meaning and promote social change from genuine and organic social problems. Rather than assuming the functionalist approach, which would be to promote the natural right of women and minorities to partake in the same benefits and blessings that our free society has to offer any other individual or group, conflict theory amplifies discord and conflict between the dominant group, which they presently define as consisting primarily of straight white men, the oppressed group consisting of and women and minorities.

Gender socialization involves the natural process by which society promotes masculinity in young men and femininity in young women. This process has been a part of every civilization and every society, without exception since the beginning of time. While historically, an element of this process has promoted inequality, this does not need to be the case. Men and women are obviously and observably different from each other biologically, for example in terms of childbearing. In the context of these differences, and while traditional societies have historically condoned inequality, the gender roles of the male and the female as partners in a family should be personal to the family as such roles should be based upon the interests and the needs of the family.

Feminist theory holds that the family is a construct that is entirely social in nature. In Marxist terms, the family structure is a form of false consciousness, a reality that was invented as a means to advance inequality and exploit the unwitting worker. The traditional conception of family is based upon a more fundamental structure which, at its core, derives from a scientific observation regarding the biological difference between the male and the female who were created by God to complement each other and to come together to procreate. The social aspect of the traditional family relationship evolved, over millennia of trial and error, into the monogamous relationship of a married man and women with children. The traditional marriage did not simply emerge out of nowhere but, over time, this organic institution became recognized, through a process of structural functionalism, as the best example of the most basic and stable social unit known to history. While the reasons for this are complex, and a study of this is beyond the scope of this book, suffice to say that there is something about the opposite nature of the male and the female, the yin and the yang to use an eastern concept, that creates a certain dynamic tension that is as unique and as creative to the married couple as is the sexual act itself. The traditional marriage would be adopted as the ideal by every major civil society and every major religion of the world.

The Exchange Theory focuses on the cost benefit aspect of the family and kinship relationships within a modern context that holds that individual need is the core value of the family and is the main factor defining the family. This theory reduces the family to nothing more than a flimsy breakable business contract as this construct strips away the significance of such virtues as commitment, love, loyalty, compassion, delayed gratification, sacrifice and, I suggest, sacredness. The Exchange Theory expresses a trend that most describes society today, a trend by which society has moved away from valuing institutional commitment. Committed relationships based upon loyalty are thus being gradually replaced by unbridled individuality which, like unbridled capitalism, is as false a paradigm as is communism. The consequence of this discernable societal trend toward Exchange Theory, to the degree by which it has been embraced as the new standard by individuals and society, has been an increase in infidelity, divorce, loveless marriage, insanity, toxic relationships, addictions, loneliness, depression, instability and a general malaise.

The Modernity Theory breaks society down into two eras. According to this theory, the first era, which starts in the Middle Ages, and ends in the 1970's, was the era that held up the traditional family as the social ideal. The second post 1970's era emphasizes the paramountcy of individual need over family or kinship groups. This idea, which has also assumed a dominant position today, coincides with the empirical disintegration of the traditional family as divorce, extra-marital families and single life has unquestionably increased since the dawning of the era that we are now in. These hedonistic times have witnessed a decline in various related institutions such as the sovereign nation-state, the institution of private property, an understanding of an objective and universal moral and ethical code, organized religion and belief in God. Paradoxically, the rise of hyper-individualism in these times, as noted by the Modernity Theory, has led to a concomitant decline in individual autonomy and political rights.

And yet, in spite of it all, the traditional family remains intact and continues to thrive as an organic institution. One of the strategies in the tool-box of the social change agents who seek to undermine the traditional family is to attack and denigrate those who dare to publicly support it. They do this with the leftist inspired array of mockery and censorship along with the usual derisive and defamatory labels. For this reason, we must answer the critique so as to not be misunderstood.

Support of the traditional family, a man and a woman in a monogamous relationship with children, is not necessarily a denigration of alternative consensual families however they may be defined. While alternative, voluntary, consensual family arrangements have and ought to have rights and ought to expect to be treated with basic dignity in a free society, nevertheless, the traditional family remains the ideal model that deserves support from all. Society holds an overall interest in preserving and promoting the traditional family as an institution whether or not we as individuals happen to be a part of such a family. We are all images of God who possess the natural right to freedom of choice within reasonable social parameters and we all hold the natural right to determine various aspects of our personal identity and our destinies within the confines of what is possible and available to us. To paraphrase Voltaire, I may disapprove of what you do, but I will defend to the death your right to do it.

The conservative theorist views life and society through the lens of what is real and what is true. Faith, reason, observation, history and science prove the obvious which is that a male is a male and a female is a female. This is provable and irrefutable science. If a person chooses, for whatever reason, to pretend they are of the other sex, or that their sex is fluid, it is their right to do so as a free individual. In the interest of manners, I would call them by whatever title they wish to be called.

This does not, however, mean that what a person calls him or herself is true. This is a complex issue where there are exceptions such as those born with elements of both sexes, a rare condition which, in those cases, one sex is favored over the other, or if an individual has a sex reassignment surgery. Other than those specific examples, those who call themselves another sex, and those who employ the culture and the state to enforce their claim, those who threaten and attack those who disagree have become part of an authoritarian leftist agenda that seeks to overthrow the conventional institutions and conventional morality, that which Karl Marx called false consciousness, institutions and ideas that include identity, reason, science, and nature and reality itself.

Critical Race Theory

Critical Theory, which is the social expression of political Marxism, has once again shape-shifted into a new form that is now known as Critical Race Theory. This theory is now being implemented in American schools, corporations, the military, law enforcement, government agencies, the judiciary and in the culture at large. Critical Race Theory is rapidly becoming a state-sponsored state mandated American philosophy, replacing the conservative philosophy that recognizes inalienable rights under God. Critical Race Theory is only the latest permutation of what could be described as a form of the cultural Marxism that began to take shape in America in the 1950's. In his book *The Death of the West,* conservative author Patrick J. Buchanan wrote about the origin of Critical Theory. He noted that while Soviet style Marxism is dead, Cultural Marxism continues onward in its long march through our institutions, our culture, our perceptions and our minds.

Critical Theory is choking our freedoms like predatory weeds choke an untended lawn. By subordinating the conservative principle of individual rights and consciousness, Critical Theory replaces the sovereign mind and intellect with a slide down the regressive rabbit hole of collective will. Critical Theory replaces the free-thinking sovereign individual with the manipulated mob by employing social and political tactics as a means to grab political and cultural advantage in what Buchanan refers to as a culture war. It is method is the Conflict Theory approach of dividing us into competing groups, which fosters group-think, and then pitting us against each other while throwing gas on the flames by emotionalizing and exploiting genuine inequalities and inequities. The insidious result of this approach, first patented by the British Fabian movement of the late 19th Century, is the barely perceptible expansion of elitist power which is imposed internally and stealthily so as to ensure that we do not become aware of our mental and spiritual enslavement.

Critical Theory achieved a major beachhead in American culture in 1933 with the establishment of The Institute for Social Research at Columbia University. Formally known as the Institute for Marxism, originally established at the Goethe Institute in Frankfurt, Germany, 1923, the Institute for Social Research developed a sociological discipline known as the Frankfurt School. The Institute for Social Research would relocate to New York when Adolf Hitler came to power in 1933. Hitler, who would implement his own social theory in Germany, embraced social theories that would, in certain respects, echo those that were embraced by the Frankfurt School. Among the theorists who emigrated to New York, all of whom would become members of the

Frankfurt School, were sociologist Wilhelm Reich, music critic Theodor Adorno, psychologist Erich Fromm and Professor Herbert Marcuse.

The self-described Marxist Frankfurt School critical theoreticians had been influenced by, among others, Italian Communist Antonio Gramsci who promoted the classic Marxist principle, as elucidated in *The Communist Manifesto* which is that the great march toward world Communism should be adapted along the way to the unique and situational conditions of the targeted society. Gramsci called for Communist theoreticians to examine each society to be targeted, to discover its weakness, and then to set up a plan to exploit those weaknesses through propaganda, agitation and subversion. Gramsci understood that the United States of America, with its traditions of freedom and private ownership, would not likely succumb to an open and bloody revolution. Gramsci determined that the most productive and road to Communism for America would involve a long and stealthy march through the cultural institutions by means of infiltration and deception.

Patrick Buchanan wrote that the social action of Critical Theory was to engage in *destructive criticism of all the main elements of Western culture, including Christianity, capitalism, authority, the family, patriarchy, hierarchy, morality, tradition, sexual restraint, loyalty, patriotism, nationalism, heredity, ethnocentrism, convention and conservatism.* Thus, the work of Critical Theory in America, in accordance with Communism, was to tear down social conventions and institutions from within while downplaying and censoring any criticism of the so-called progressive societies. By this means, terror in the Soviet Union, Red China and other nations chafing under the jack-boot of the progressive Communist social experiment would be blamed on Capitalism and specifically on the United States.

One sociological manifestation of Critical Theory is Cultural Pessimism which is manifested by a kneejerk loathing of everything American. Indeed, the newly minted anti-American, having fallen under the spell of Critical Theory, enters into a state of denial over advantages that he or she might enjoy as a result of being American. As is often the case, the more privileged the person may be, the more likely they might be swayed by this aspect of Critical Theory. The privileged adherent, it has been suggested, might suffer from pangs of guilt over their own privilege which they believe they do not deserve. Certainly, they have the option to redistribute their own surplus, and yet very few choose this. They instead choose to spurn the opportunity to get relief from their feelings of guilt as they project that guilt onto the rest of us.

It is true that in our imperfect society Americans are born into various levels of advantage and dis-advantage. A child of the Rockefeller family is born into greater privilege than is a child of poverty. We should acknowledge that there is a racial component to this inequity as our institutions and our government has historically put the proverbial thumb on the scale in terms of advantaging some individuals and groups over others. African-Americans have obviously not been treated equally in America and have been deprived of equity as a result of policies of racism and discrimination.

Critical Theory exploits these shameful facts of history by stoking hatred for the system, as imperfect as it may be, that nevertheless offers the only real hope of redemption from those artificially imposed systems of inequality. State sponsored racism and discrimination against African-Americans, along with the historic mistreatment of Native-Americans, represents a long and disgraceful history of government and societal involvement in social experimentation that sought to deprive the inalienable rights of every citizen under God. Racism, described by philosopher and author Ayn Rand as a primitive form of socialism, is a stain on America and on much of the world. Examples of more recent government sponsored social engineering include programs based upon eugenics, a movement that was all the rage with the left until World War II made it unfashionable and drove it underground, the use of state-sponsored psychiatry to commit thousands of non-conforming women to mental hospitals and the placement of abortion clinics in black neighborhoods as a means to cull those who social engineer Margaret Sanger described as members of dysgenic races.

Social scientist Wilhelm Reich, viewed as one of the founders of the modern sexual revolution, studied the means by which Marxism and Psychology could be intermingled and how Marxism could be further cloaked in the garment of social science as opposed to as a political idea. By this means, the science of psychology has been routinely used to attack and discredit conservatives as mentally ill and to attack conservatism as a form of mental repression. Reich theorized that the separation of sexuality from traditional moral restraint might lead to the development of a more degraded individual who, as such, would be less attached to institutions and ideas that promote freedom, institutions that he believed fostered inequality which he viewed as anathema. Reich, who had joined the Communist Party of Germany in 1930, worked with Sigmund Freud at a time when he was developing his theory of polymorphous perversity. Reich, who isolated sexuality from its moral context, claimed to use science to explain sexuality and he contributed toward politicizing psychology in a manner similar to the way Darwin used scientific theory to codify and further enable racism.

In his magnum opus, *The Mass Psychology of Fascism,* Wilhelm Reich theorized that the middle-class family, under his assumption that the family was an artificial construct and was an institution manufactured by an authoritarian system, was a *reactionary germ cell* residing at the foundation of fascism. This thesis was further elaborated upon by fellow Frankfurt School theoretician Theodor Adorno who, in his book *The Authoritarian Personality* claimed that an individual who embraced middle class, conservative Christian values was, de facto, a fascist and a racist. Patrick Buchanan quoted Wisconsin conservative radio host and senior fellow at the Wisconsin Policy Research Center Charles Sykes who referred to Adorno's book, which is considered by many to be the *altarpiece of the Frankfurt School,* as *presenting an uncompromising indictment of bourgeois civilization, with the twist that what was considered merely old-fashioned by previous critics was now declared both fascistic and psychologically warped.*

The libelous indictment of the American people by the Frankfurt School critical theorists is mildly comparable to the pseudo-scientific racist arguments used by their contemporaries, the Nazis, in their accusations against the Jews. The Frankfurt School critical theorists launched the tactic of psychological conditioning as a bludgeon against American conservatives, or for that matter as a weapon against anyone who dissented from the party line as anyone who fell afoul of their authoritarian vision could be declared mentally ill and in need of treatment. This approach was also standard procedure for the Soviets who sent those who they deemed to have mental maladies to Siberia or to the gulag for sensitivity training or re-education. Buchanan, in *The Death of the West*, referred to the Frankfurt School as having established the *therapeutic state* where *sin is redefined as sickness, crime becomes antisocial behavior, and the psychiatrist replaces the priest.*

The critical theorist considered to be the grand poobah of the Frankfurt School was Brandeis Professor Herbert Marcuse who was referred to as one of the pied pipers of the 1960's counter-culture. Buchanan noted that Marcuse fostered the development of *radical youth, feminists, black militants, homosexuals, the alienated, the asocial, Third World revolutionaries, all the angry voices of the persecuted 'victims' of the West.* In his book *Eros and Civilization,* Marcuse openly promoted sex, drugs, polymorphous perversity, rock and roll, and an open rejection of the western social canon. Coining the slogan *Make Love not War*, Marcuse was a cult figure amongst college leftists.

Conventional wisdom might consider Marcuse and the elitist college radicals that he inspired to have been supporters of freedom and individual rights, but this support for freedom only applied to freedom from moral constraint. Marcuse's book, *One Dimensional Man,* spilled the beans on the leftist agenda in its call for an *educational dictatorship* to be controlled by critical theorists and by those who were properly conditioned by them, those to whom we might today refer to as woke. In this influential tome, Marcuse wrote about *repressive tolerance* by which colleges and public schools and institutions would persecute conservatives while tolerating the left. I need not state the obvious by observing that, in the real sense, Marcuse was a secular prophet.

Marcuse and his merry troupe of critical theorists, contemporaries of Stalin who implemented his own version of Critical Theory in Russia, were aware of the dictate that Stalin published in 1943. We should note that Stalin and the international radical left that followed the Bolshevik lead, had been pro-Hitler from the time of the August 23, 1939, signing of the Hitler-Stalin Pact, which launched World War II, up until June 22, 1941, two years later, when Germany invaded Russia and Hitler double-crossed his socialist ally. Stalin's declaration established the party line at a time when the tide had turned, and the Soviets knew they would win the war. The Soviets would thus shift gears and come out against the United States, their erstwhile ally of convenience. Stalin's declaration remains at the core of the pro-Communist strategy today: *Members and front organizations must continually embarrass, discredit, and degrade our critics. When obstructionists become too irritating, label them as fascist, or Nazi or anti-Semitic…The association will, after enough repetition, become 'fact' in the public mind.*

Conflict Theory turns morality into a political football as morality becomes something invented by whoever is in power. Critical Theory applies a moral ax to the bifurcated half of society deemed to be the exploiter while erasing moral standards for the so-called exploited. At the core of Critical Theory, and at the core of the entire Communist enterprise, is the nihilistic notion that there is no morality but rather, that morality is a construct manufactured by those in power. This is why the left is all about power as everything in the universe becomes dependent on the secular control of the power to invent truth. The conservative, in contrast, seeks to discover and build upon an objective knowledge of a real as well as an abstract source of morality, a source that exists outside the cloudy and imperfect lens of human perception and the biased hand of human manipulation, a source that, as such, would apply to all equally.

The social theory of Micro-aggression was formulated within the context of Conflict Theory by Psychiatrist and Harvard Medical School Professor Chester M. Pierce in 1970. Dr. Pierce, the first African-American professor to work at Massachusetts General Hospital, was the author of over 180 books, articles and reviews. His micro-aggression theory expanded the definition of racism to include subconsciously derived behaviors or actions that might be considered racist in their orientation. This theory would subjectively place a proverbial microscope over any comment or action that might be taken to contain racial undertones whether deliberate, culturally ingrained, or subconscious. While the theory itself is a valid look at the individual and society, in the hands of critical theorists with their authoritarian orientation that leans toward, as Marcuse described it, *educational dictatorship*, microaggression becomes repression and tyranny.

Micro-aggression offers a scientific veneer to a new definition of racism when viewed in the context of the Frankfurt School. In this context, a micro-aggression can only be committed by a so-called exploiter or, arbitrarily, by anyone perceived to be a political enemy of the clique of leftists in power and that might include fellow leftists who might threaten or challenge power. Thus, micro-aggression becomes corrupted by a political agenda as opposed to being merely a scientific theory worthy of objective research. In this context, a person or group classified as exploited cannot commit a micro-aggression as micro-aggression is a hammer to be exclusively used to destroy dissent. Micro-aggressions committed by the exploited class or by their elitist overlords in the ruling establishment, and that would include real racists, are either ignored or swept under the rug.

The politicizing of science is a phenomena that has corrupted a surprisingly wide range of otherwise legitimate scientific disciplines. It should be noted that the conservative scientific approach, which the left seeks to demonize with the label *anti-science*, is to separate science and politics as much as possible so as to not corrupt its mission which is to derive truths from nature and to harness that which has been learned so as to improve life on earth. Conservatives seek to rightfully integrate moral and ethical standards into scientific research so as to restrain scientific disciplines such as nuclear research, experimentation on human beings, and Gain of Function research as took place at the Institute of Virology in Wuhan, China, supported by Dr. Anthony Fauci which, according to most scientists, caused the COVID 19 Pandemic.

The most recent manifestation of the ongoing shape-shifting saga that is Critical Theory is contained in the 1619 Project. Published in the August 18, 2019, issue of The New York Times Magazine, the 1619 Project now serves as an informal manual for what has become known as Critical Race Theory. The 1619 Project, written by liberal and leftist academics, journalists and artists, begins with the audacious announcement that the real date of America's birth was not July 4, 1776, the date that the Declaration of Independence was published, but in late August 1619 when a slave ship landed at Point Comfort, on the coast of the British colony of Virginia, with 20-30 enslaved Africans on board.

Right out of the gate, this assertion regarding the founding of the American Republic is false which goes to the overall artificial nature of the leftist enterprise. When objective reality does not exist, when existence itself is viewed as to be in the eye of the beholder, an enlightened elite must step into the vacuum to fill the void of unreality as people need to know truths in order to be alive and avoid insanity. We must have a structure by which we determine truths and falsehoods, and this structure must be affixed to a set point in time and space. This aspect of every human being is baked into our nature. Thus, a void develops from not recognizing an external God as the creator of truth or, for the atheist, nature and natures god. This void is filled by an earthly elite, whether that elite is in the form of a charismatic and godlike surrogate like Hitler or Stalin, or whether the definer of truth is an article published in the New York Times Magazine, one that is turned into a state-sponsored philosophy. Indeed, a refusal to accept the new truth could cause negative consequences for the dissenter.

The premise of the 1619 Project is correct in that slavery is evil, that the history of slavery and racism in America has not been fully told or understood and the inequities that have emanated out of that history have not been fully addressed. Conservative social theory applies a different analysis to those central questions than does Critical Race Theory. Slavery, an evil institution that should be categorized in the same social grouping as would be human sacrifice, idol worship, cannibalism and rape, involved the primitive idea that one human being had a right to own another human being as one would own any other form of property. The Bible has been criticized for recognizing slavery, but this should be viewed in context. In biblical times, institutions such as private property, business ownership and individual rights were in their initial stages of development. Back then, the collectivist notion of the tribe was the predominant social structure and slavery was the primary institution of labor. Tribes, often at war with each other, would enslave members of the defeated side and would rape their women. This was standard practice all over the world and slavery was the last vestige of these types of institutions to fall out of favor and to go by the wayside in terms of social acceptance.

Conservatives understand that the Bible reflects social realities as they existed in ancient times. Yet the Bible began the process of reforming such beliefs and practices in the context of what was possible in those times as the Bible was the first document in recorded history that called for the banning of human sacrifice, idol worship, activities around idol worship and cannibalism. While the Bible did not ban slavery outright, the Bible nevertheless began to regulate slavery which set the stage, over subsequent millennia, for its eventual abolition by the biblically oriented West. The Bible, for the first time in history, by regulating slavery, recognized that slaves were full human beings with basic specific rights.

When the 1619 Project claims that the arrival of African slaves in Virginia marked the beginning of America, the 1619 Project ignores the simultaneous development in America of an abolitionist movement, particularly in the northern colonies. That abolitionist movement was based upon Calvinist principles that were established by the Puritans in New England as well as the Quakers of Pennsylvania as well as various other Protestant sects. The abolitionist movement, originating in New England, was the first movement in history that sought to abolish the immoral and barbaric institution of slavery on religious and moral grounds. Indeed, the African-American church, which has always been, and which remains a great moral force in America, a moral engine that inspires and continues to energize American Christianity overall, drew its inspiration, and still does, from the Calvinism of the Puritan founders.

A proper examination of history and society in a historical context requires what Sociologist C. Wright Mills called a Sociological Imagination and this discipline requires an opening of the lens in order to place society in a wider context to grasp a bigger picture. In terms of American slavery, this would require a context that would include an examination of slavery as an institution in the world at the time, particularly in the Americas Africa and Asia. While a deep examination of this fascinating topic is beyond the scope of this book, suffice to say that the number of slaves that were imported into the colonies that would become the United States was a small fraction of the total imported into the Americas. It has been estimated that the average number imported into what would become the United States was about 3% of the total. Another fascinating topic, beyond the scope of this book but one worthy of deep study, was the Arab enslavement of Africans and the involvement of African kingdoms in the slave trade with Portuguese, Spanish, French, Dutch and British ships plying their sinister and immoral trade off the African coast.

While it is certainly appropriate for the 1619 Project to focus on the history of slavery in the United States and the ongoing impact of slavery and racism on African-Americans and on American society, and while an honest and unvarnished history of African slavery and of African-Americans is a key component in terms of knowing who we are as Americans and how we got here, and while there is much good to be found in the 1619 Project, the lack of nuance and context is, I would nevertheless suggest, part and parcel of a Critical Theory approach which views, as examples, such subjects as the history of African and Arab slavery as the story of an oppressed people to be therefore ignored. This approach also avoids even a brief examination of slavery elsewhere in the Americas so as to not distract from a thesis that is marred by an anti-American political agenda.

The 1619 Project claims that *one of the primary reasons the colonists decided to declare their independence from Britain was to protect the institution of slavery* (Nikole Hannah Jones, p. 18.) There is not a shred of evidence to back up this audacious claim. Indeed, the colony of Georgia prohibited slavery when it was founded by James Oglethorpe in 1733 and

Georgia was forced to accept slavery by an occupying British militia in 1752. While Thomas Jefferson has been criticized for being a slaveowner, nevertheless, and paradoxically, Jefferson's Declaration of Independence, of which the original draft condemned slavery outright, set the stage for its eventual abolition with his revolutionary assertion that all men are created equal. By establishing the political philosophy of the new American Republic as based upon this biblical principle, of equality under the creator, Jefferson, who was extremely conflicted regarding slavery, nevertheless should be viewed as having set the stage for its eventual abolition.

At the time of the American Revolution, abolitionist movements were developing in all of the colonies and the abolition of slavery had already occurred in several northern colonies starting with the colony of Rhode Island. Several of our founding fathers, including Alexander Hamilton and Gouverneur Morris, were abolitionists and the question of slavery was hotly debated during the constitutional convention of 1787-1788. The missing aspect of the 1619 Project in this regard is that while slavery was preserved in the southern states, as a result of a compromise that avoided civil war and led to the ratification of the Constitution and the American Republic in 1789, and while this was and remains a moral stain, the northern American states were, nevertheless, the first governments in world history to abolish the barbarous institution of slavery by law. For this reason, this period of American history might be viewed in the context of conservative social theory as a glass half full and as a work in progress as opposed to the critical theory approach which is as a glass half empty.

The 1619 Project claims: *The wealth and prominence that allowed Jefferson, at just thirty-three, and the other founding fathers to believe they could successfully break off from one of the mightiest empires in the world came from the dizzying profits generated by chattel slavery.* (Nikole Hannah Jones, p. 18)   This is an exaggeration that dismisses the growth of the non-slave economies of the northern states with their emerging manufacturing, trade, and small businesses as factors contributing to the wealth of the country. While it is true that slave labor on southern plantations did develop a wealthy and authoritarian slavocracy in southern states, economically this model led to a weakening of those economies and left most average southerners in poverty.

The 1619 Project is similar in its agenda to *A People's History of the United States* by the late social scientist and Boston University Professor Howard Zinn. Published in 1980, Zinn's book continues to have an enormous impact on American high school and college students where it is still often assigned reading in political science courses. Like the 1619 Project, Zinn's book is filled with fascinating factoids as it offers the reader the thrilling feeling of delving into forbidden and secret history. While both works are filled with vital information that has been often obscured by the mainstream culture, both are filled with serious errors, exaggerations, and half-truths in the service of a leftist ideology.

The sociological imagination requires us to look beyond an ideological vision of history and society, to integrate valuable information into a wholistic understanding. This means that a narrative should be balanced, that it should offer contrasting views and that it should include nuance. Those qualities are lacking in the 1619 Project and in the works of Howard Zinn. Certainly, any analysis, including this one, holds degrees of bias. Any analysis is subject to the limitations of the information that is available at the time it is developed, and any analysis is influenced by the times, the society and various circumstances. The 1619 Project and Zinn's history have a lot to offer the reader as a whole which is why it is too bad; they are warped by an ideological agenda. There is nothing wrong with an activist driven theory, per se, but such theory should be viewed in that context and, as such, should not be accepted as doctrine. The conservative approach to social theory involves an attempt to offer balance, within the context of bias, in its quest to discover the truths that reside between the extremes.

The 1619 Project offers an accurate and unvarnished history of the wrongs and atrocities that the African-American community endured in the United States. The sociological imagination would place that history in the context of examining American philosophy, society and politics in the times described and, overall, as they were and as they are. Certainly, American society and government has historically been de-facto white supremacist and yet an overall examination of America would indicate that this was never, to paraphrase the late great Rev. Dr. Martin Luther King, the true meaning of our creed.

We should apply the same sociological imagination to the Nazi Holocaust against the Jews of Europe. A literal study of that atrocity, and the ongoing promotion of those facts in all of its ugly detail is a crucial factor both in terms of knowing history and in terms of preventing such an evil event from ever occurring again. The sociological imagination might open the lens and examine not only what was going on in Germany in the decades leading up to the Holocaust, but such an examination ought to include the philosophy and the politics of Nazism as a means to understand the root causes of the Holocaust. I would theorize that the philosophy and the governing principle of Nazism, which set the stage for the Holocaust, was socialism as defined within a hyper-nationalist and internationalist context.

This broad and complex history is beyond the scope of this book. I have written more extensively on this topic in previous books listed in the bibliography. Suffice to say that Nazism is National Socialism with all that this implies including the centralized authoritarian state, hero worship, utopianism and the elimination of those labeled by the state as enemies of the people which, in the case of Nazi Germany, was the Jews. The Jews were portrayed by the Nazis as having ripped off working people which set the stage for the confiscation of their property. The rhetoric used in this regard, as an examination of public statements made by Hitler and other prominent Nazis indicates, have echoes found within the rhetoric of class envy that is routinely used by liberal and left-wing American politicians today. The Jews were portrayed by the Nazis as an inferior race by means of the Darwinian idea of evolving and devolving races, or species, an idea which was the state philosophy of the Nazis, and an idea which they used as a substitute for the Judeo-Christian concept that all human beings are created equally in the image of God. The Nazis and the Communists were competing so-called progressive social and political experiments each fighting the other while finding commonalities in practice. Indeed, much of the Nazi infrastructure, the national police known as the Gestapo, the concentration camps, the perpetual war, the genocide, was built upon observations of the system that had been put in place previously by the so-called progressive V. I. Lenin, head of the Communist Bolsheviks in nearby Russia.

Thus, I would argue, a sociological examination of Nazi Germany and, for that matter, of Soviet Russia yields the obvious conclusion that those systems were false, evil, irredeemable and rotten to the core. This observation, I would argue, is not the case with the American system even though we as a nation engaged in atrocities against African-Americans and Native-Americans that were, indeed, comparable to those engaged in by the two great Socialist experiments of the 20th Century. While as Americans we ought to understand the history of slavery, racism and discrimination, we should do so as a means to live up to the true meaning of our creed, a creed which is righteous. We might also note that the Nazi and Communist social experiments led to a resurgence of a form of slavery in our own time, a slavery where all citizens, except a small elite group of party members, as property of the state that they are forced to serve.

We should study our history as a means toward evolving into a more perfect union as opposed to as a means toward tearing down our union. Critical Theory, to reiterate, is an agenda meant to tear down America as, historically, the critical theorists rarely criticized Communism and only criticized Nazism when it suited their situational goals. Conservative social theory views an American philosophy as holding that the citizen is endowed by God, or by the creator, with inalienable rights. Our creed as individual citizens is a vision of the citizen thriving in a sovereign land of farmers, small business owners, inventors, small corporations, entrepreneurs, creators, teachers, laborers, all offering their services on the free market and all enjoying the blessings and benefits of private ownership, of free institutions and of the limited government that our forebears devised as a means to protect those God given freedoms.

Critical Theory views society within a negative collectivist context first and foremost. Critical Theory subjects the individual to a group identity that might contain a mix of hackneyed stereotypes and preconceived notions, some of which may have been invented by the critical theorist, notions that may or may not apply to the individual so labeled. Critical Theory ignores the centrality of the conscious individual while emphasizing collective association. Critical Theory exists within the context of the Conflict Theory dialectic of collectives pitted against each other as a means to develop further collectivization and a surrender of consciousness and freedom. The conservative views collective association as a voluntary matter and as a secondary definition in terms of defining a person. The conservative holds the value of the individual under God, under natures god, as the first definition of who a person is and how a person develops character. The second consideration is the value of the family and an immediate circle of friends and associates. The third includes the value of work, avocation, community, religion, politics, pastimes, and ethnic identity. The forth is loyalty to country and to a national language, culture and custom.

As this book goes to press, Critical Race Theory is playing out within our cultural institutions, our corporations, our military and particularly within our schools in a manner that has never been as blatant and as visible as it is today. Karl Marx, along with America's primary founder of so-called progressive education John Dewey understood that the best way to transform a society is to control the minds of its children through education. Critical Race Theory is now collectivizing our young children by means of dividing them by race and ethnic background and then by pitting each side against the other. Black children are taught that to succeed in America, to excel in science, the humanities, business, is to act white and, as such, to sell out to the racist system that is America. White children are taught to not excel as to do so means that they are becoming a part of white privilege. Both black and white children are taught that America is inherently evil, and that America is irredeemable, that white people are inherently racist as if this were biological. While our children are being coerced into identifying themselves based on their race, at the same time the most basic and fundamental of all categories, the most scientific category, the one that exists in nature, the one that the animal kingdom understands which is the difference between the two sexes, is being blurred and is being airbrushed out of existence.

It is not enough for the left to declare religion and the nation-state as a myth and an anachronism invented by exploiters, as we will discuss in the next chapter, but now, the existence of the separate and distinct male and female no longer exists according to them. Our children are now being taught that masculinity and femininity are inventions, that these aspects of human nature are unnatural and are inherently toxic and that the good progressive should erase these factors from their minds. Both the race theories which, in a different context, were introduced into the Nazi school system after Hitler came to power, and the new theories of sexuality may be enough to cause eventual conditions of insanity and social disorder in our younger generation which is one of the goals of the agenda behind these twisted teachings. All of this is occurring at a time when children are required to cover their faces with pieces of cloth in a manner that is not dissimilar to, in a different context, girls who live in radicalized Islamic societies who must do likewise.

As this book goes to press, the leftist and, as such, the authoritarian oriented Biden Administration is openly exposing its fangs regarding the coerced installation of these new modalities of education in public schools. Mothers and fathers are now showing up in droves at local school board hearings and they are speaking up, in no uncertain terms, regarding their opposition to these methods of teaching. Attorney General Merrick Garland, responding to a request from the leftist National School Boards Association, which seeks to silence their opposition, has asked the FBI to consider categorizing these moms and dads who are speaking up against Critical Race Theory as *Domestic Terrorists*. Meanwhile, AG Garland's son in law, Xan Tanner, co-founded a company called Panorama Education which is one of the primary providers of Critical Race Theory. Panorama, with backing from Mark Zuckerberg, founder of Facebook, represents a conflict of interest for AG Garland, it has been argued, as he criminalizes the opposition to Critical Race Theory while his family benefits financially.

Increasing numbers of Americans are growing in awareness regarding the insidious agenda of Critical Race Theory and Americans are demanding that this form of Marxism be replaced by conservative social theory in education. Americans seek social theory that more accurately reflects the American political and social philosophy and American values. Americans want educational disciplines and the teaching of modes of thinking that help children to think independently, to know who they are and to know what they seek in life as a result of that mode of thinking. Americans want their children to be better equipped in terms of developing independent, moral, and successful lives on their own terms.

The Grand Conspiracy

The word conspiracy comes from the Latin word *conspire* which means to breathe together, to unite, to plot. A conspiracy may take place when two or more people join together in secret in order to hatch a plot to engage in something evil, criminal or subversive. Certainly, criminal conspiracies happen all the time. These sorts of events do not usually just simply happen by accident, nor are they usually the action of one single lone actor. Such events require levels of planning and coordination that usually involves more than one person.

A criminal conspiracy might involve either a small cell or a large syndicate such as the Mafia. Such a syndicate may develop informal control over aspects of a targeted society through a combination of terror and the illicit use of ill-gotten gains for bribery and, at times, for social services as a means to buy favor and create dependency. One of my fellow classmates at Bunker Hill Community College, an Italian national, recently described his life growing up in Sicily. He noted that people in Sicily and in portions of Southern Italy tend to avoid getting into business out of fear of the Mafia which has formed an informal and secretive government. The Mafia has become so entrenched and so powerful in that region of Italy that no person or group, including the government in Rome, is able to take them down.

Nations establish independent systems of justice as a means to expose and combat such criminal conspiracies. One of the main purposes of free speech and a free press is to provide an independent means by which the average citizen might investigate criminal conspiracies and expose their findings to the public. Emanating from such exposure, our system of justice might step in with police investigation and arrests when warranted. When enough evidence of criminality is uncovered, our court system might step in with a trial by which evidence might be judged by a jury which renders judgement and justice.

Political conspiracies also happen. Indeed, whenever and wherever power and wealth exists there will always be those of criminal intent, those who seek to take dishonest advantage by criminal means, those who will conspire with others to pull off an outcome that favors their position. Political conspiracies are usually more complex than are criminal conspiracies as they involve the attainment of power and influence as opposed to merely the attainment of property and money.

Bad conspiracy theories involve claims that religious or ethnic groups participate in a conspiracy. This is impossible on its face. It is impossible for millions of people, or even for tens of thousands of people to be involved in a secret plot to engage in criminal or subversive behavior. Such bad conspiracy theories have often involved claims against the Jews, but these types of claims might crop up against any group at any time. The target of such conspiracy theories is usually a minority within a society. The modus operandi of this type of conspiracy theory is stoking distrust and fear of the *other*.

This type of conspiracy theorizing is known to social scientists as scapegoating. This is more likely to occur when a society is experiencing social or economic stress and is more vulnerable to the easy cheap approach of blaming some group that is perceived to be outside the mainstream for the problems that the society is experiencing. This type of false conspiracy theorizing becomes particularly lethal when weaponized by an elite clinging to power, an elite seeking control over the official organs of propaganda and the machinery of government as this was the case with Adolf Hitler. Such self-serving and destructive demagoguery tends to deflect attention away from the true locus of culpability.

Indeed, those in positions of power, both in government and in the private sector, might from time to time cook up specific conspiracy theories as a means to discredit and damage their opposition. In this sense, they conspire to create and disseminate a conspiracy theory. This happens all the time in politics and during political campaigns. A classic example of this type of conspiracy theorizing was the claim that candidate and then President Donald Trump was spying for Russia. This conspiracy theory, cooked up by a small group operating within the FBI, the DOJ under President Barack Obama and the Hillary Clinton campaign received the full backing of a vast array of both witting and unwitting media outlets and this plot was used to harass and distract the Trump Administration during Trump's first three years in office.

Specific conspiracy theories differ from an overall conspiratorial mindset. In the mid-19th Century, two such conspiratorial mindsets began to take shape, and both continue to define elements of the societal and individual outlook today. The conspiratorial mindset of the left was consolidated by Karl Marx and its most influential text remains the 1848 *Communist Manifesto*. The conspiratorial mindset of conservatism more naturally emerged out of the ideas and thinking of the American founding generation. Both schools of thought, hold kernels of truth within them while both may lead to warped societal and personal views when held in extreme forms. Both schools of thought, at their extreme, hold anti-Semitic opinions within the context of each of their respective forms.

The overall leftist conspiratorial viewpoint is based upon a corruption by Marx of the dialectical theory that was developed early in the 19th Century by German philosopher Georg Wilhelm Friedrich Hegel who had been, in turn, inspired by the thinking of the late 18th Century philosopher Immanuel Kant. Proposing that society was bifurcated into two spheres, Kant viewed society as divided into the nominal and the phenomenal world. According to Kant, the nominal world is the known world, which is an illusion, and the phenomenal world, which is the real world, is unknowable to human perception. The Bible and science recognize elements of nature that are dialectically opposite to each other, that conflict, interaction and combination between these elements represents forces of energy, and that the Bible views aspects a spiritual realm that is unknowable to mankind.

Marx applied the dialectic of Hegel to the social and political order by dividing society into two spheres, the Bourgeoisie and the Proletariat. Marx viewed these two spheres as in a perpetual clash with each other, what he called the class struggle. Hegel had devised the dialectical idea of a thesis and an antithesis clashing with each other until both eventually destroyed the other and a new synthesis would then emerge out of the detritus. The new synthesis would then again become divided into two warring spheres until another more advanced and refined synthesis would emerge. The final synthesis, the ushering in of the secular messianic age of perfection, a time when conflict ends, when humankind is harmoniously merged with nature and the universe, is a condition that Marx called Communism.

The conspiratorial viewpoint of the left is thus based upon the dialectical conflict between the Bourgeoisie and the Proletariat economic classes. Marx viewed the dialectical conflict between the two spheres as unbalanced with the wealthier and the more capitalist Bourgeoisie exploiting and expropriating from the victimized Proletariat class of workers and toilers. Marx claimed that material wealth was solely created by the Proletariat and that this wealth was then confiscated by the Bourgeoisie through conspiracy and trickery. Marx claimed that the Bourgeoisie held the power, by means of their confiscation of undeserved wealth, to shape reality in order to oppress the Proletariat through force and deception by means of creating what Marx called false consciousness. Ideas that Marx claimed constituted false consciousness, ideas that he claimed were invented by the Bourgeoisie as means to exploit the Proletariat, included self-interest, love, loyalty, faith and competition. Marx viewed such social institutions as religion, family, the nation-state, borders, private property, free trade, and any institution that he viewed as fostering inequality as entities and institutions manufactured by the Bourgeoisie as forms of false consciousness. These ideas, Marx claimed, were invented in order to suppress the perceptions of the true creators of wealth, the workers of the world.

This is the basis of the conspiracy theory of exploitation by which the Bourgeoisie conspires to rip off the Proletariat. Marx theory was based upon the struggle of the economic classes which did not allow for a middle class. In fact, communism did not acknowledge the existence of a middle class as the early Communists would only refer to a *middle strata*. The theory of exploitation expanded to include a dialectic of race and geography as a result of the social theories of 20th Century French West Indian Communist Psychiatrist Frantz Fannon, author of *The Wretched of the Earth*, published in 1961. Fanon's dialectical theory is expressed today as Critical Theory. This is why many leftists, imbued with a conspiratorial outlook that it provides the foundation of their worldview and their understanding of reality, feel that *the millionaires and the billionaires*, to coin a phrase popularized by Massachusetts Senator Elizabeth Warren, or greedy corporations and the rich have ripped them off and are somehow responsible for all the social ills of the world as well as many of their own personal problems.

The conspiracy theory of the left, as manifested in its more extreme forms, holds Jews as key players in their conspiracy of exploitation. This is because Jews and Judaism, in this hagiography, represents capitalism, private ownership, individual initiative, education, faith, and other ideas and institutions that stand in the way of Marx fantasy of a one world Communist ant colony. Marx was very explicit about this in his once famous 1845 pamphlet *On the Jewish Question*, a pamphlet that was re-published in the late 19th Century as *A World without Jews*. The theme of Marx infamous pamphlet, one which blamed the Jews for capitalism, was a standard part of leftist education until Hitler made such expression unfashionable and Stalin employed the charge of anti-Semitism as a hammer against his enemies. This type of conspiracy thinking has been partially transferred by some leftists into conspiratorial claims regarding the State of Israel. I would suggest that leftists who despise Israel today have resurrected Marx thesis in *On the Jewish Question* with elements of hatred toward national sovereignty and belief in God, all of which, they tend to believe, constitute an updated understanding of false consciousness.

The conservative conspiratorial viewpoint is more selective and specific with claims that an informal secretive elite, one that has expanded globally since the 19th Century, one that is founded upon a network of secret societies, tends to subversively control or to at least influence most of the nations, cultures and economies of the world. The conservative conspiracy theory does not include any particular religion or ethnic group, nor does it include an economic class, but conservatives tend to claim that the conspiracy consists of a small and informal network of well-placed top-level elite figures and secretive organizations that hold access to wealth and power over the major organizations and institutions of the world both inside and outside of governments. The conservative theory holds that the general philosophy of the members of this network leans toward combinations of Atheism, Satanism, or toward some secretive new-age type cult. The politics of this secretive cabal, according to this theory, seeks to control and manage an all-encompassing unelected and unofficial world government.

Secret societies have been around since time immemorial and, as such, secret societies are a natural and normal part of any society. Secret societies are part and parcel of the natural right to privacy and are recognized in the constitution as the right to assemble. Secret transactions and communications are rightfully protected by law and custom as, for example, secrecy is codified into law regarding lawyer-client privilege, the right to privacy regarding doctor and patient, privacy in marriage, non-disclosure contracts in business, the confidentiality agreement between cleric and parishioner.

Secret societies have played positive roles in history as was the case with the Sons of Liberty, the secretive masonic oriented group that hatched the Boston Tea Party as secrecy was required in order to hatch that plot. Claus von Stauffenberg secretly conspired with other high level Nazi officials to assassinate Hitler on July 20, 1944. A certain level of secrecy in both our professional and personal lives is required and is a natural element in the functioning of a free person in a free society and, as such, secrecy is a basic function of freedom.

And yet…secret societies, due to their secretive nature, are more prone to corruption as secrecy might be employed in the service of either good or bad. In this regard, good or bad intent and good or bad activity when planned and conducted in secret might become magnified either way depending upon the wealth, the size, the power and the connections of the society in question. Of particular concern would be secret societies that require oaths of allegiance to the society over all other people and things including family and country.

For these complex reasons, and within the context of moderation and with respect for the right to assemble and the right to secrecy, I embrace an understanding of the conservative conspiracy theory. I would suggest that by the late 19th Century, the secret societies of the West had reached an international level of intersectionality, power and influence. While it is virtually impossible to penetrate the inner secrets of these societies, and while there is great dispute in terms of which groups are part of this network, enough factors are identifiable in terms of understanding aspects of their nature and agenda to the degree that we can discern, with more than educated guesses, what they might be up to.

I believe that the cornerstone of the philosophy of this secretive network is an atheistic belief by their membership, imbued with a sense of privilege and noblesse oblige, which causes them an undue sense of guilt that in turn manifests as a held belief that they have an obligation to control and transform all of human society. They embrace a communistic vision, one that has been historically expressed in such seminal documents as *The Communist Manifesto*, the *Twenty-Five Points of the Nazi Party* and *The Humanist Manifesto*. They view the Theory of Evolution, Charles Darwin's call to arms which is biological advancement, as the founding tenet of their secular faith, a tenet that leads them toward coercive power in the service of evolving mankind into a new and superior species while slowly winnowing out those they perceive as weak or into regressive ideas that stand in the way of their version of progress. They are sincere in their belief in their right to hold power over the planet for what they believe is for the common good. They believe that they hold mystic possession of a higher cosmic form of consciousness.

Conservative social theory indicates that any study of the grand conspiracy or of secret societies should involve caution, sagacity, serious scholarship and exacting standards of proof. Due to the secretive nature of the grand conspiracy itself it is difficult to truly know the inner workings of the conspiracy or whether or not secret societies, in and of themselves, might have been the source of false conspiracy theories. Right off the bat, any conspiracy theory that involves the Jews or any other religious or ethnic group, or any large group or movement per se, should be dismissed as a self-serving theory that was at least fueled if not manufactured by true conspirators who seek to exploit collective fear, bigotry and other base elements of human emotion. Conspirators who may control governments are themselves more often than not behind this type of conspiracy speculation as they benefit from fanning the flames of hate. This method has historically served the interests of demagogues who seek to consolidate power through fear and the marshalling of hate as they confiscate the property, commit atrocities and, in extreme cases, commit genocide against the group they libel.

By employing the sociological imagination, we begin to examine the grand conspiracy, that which Whittaker Chambers, the former American communist who testified at the Hiss Trial in the late 1940's described as a conspiracy of gentlemen, by documenting evidence and examining the impact of that conspiracy, philosophically and politically, on our societies and on individual life historically and today. It should be noted that what we might define as a grand conspiracy might be considered to represent social and political progress by some and might be viewed as honest and as wholesome by others which means that such an identification of conspiracy holds a level of subjectivity. I acknowledge that my examination of what constitutes a grand conspiracy is conducted through the lens of conservative social theorizing and analysis.

A study of the grand conspiracy and of secret societies before the 18th Century is a fascinating and important exercise. My contention is that versions of the grand conspiracy have always existed in human society. Conspiracy is, indeed, normal and natural to society. Please keep in mind that any study of the history of conspiracy will reveal vast and legitimate differences of opinion and the truth is often hard to discern given the secretive nature of the conspiracy itself.

I contend that the modern grand conspiracy was hatched during the 1793-1795 Reign of Terror in France. The late Dr. James H. Billington, Professor of History at Harvard and Princeton Universities, 13th Librarian of Congress, one of America's most respected scholars authored *Fire in the Minds of Men, Origins of the Revolutionary Faith,* where he documented a conspiracy that subverted the otherwise democratic and American inspired French Revolution of 1789. Dr. Billington traced the conspiracy to the Illuminati, founded in Bavaria on July 4, 1776, by Canon Law Professor Adam Weishaupt. A conventional study of the secretive Jacobin regime in France, which Billington connects to the Illuminati, and which launched what is known as the Reign of Terror, reveals in stark and indisputable terms what I describe as the agenda of the grand conspiracy in broad daylight. The Jacobin regime was based upon the principle of a communistic world government that would attempt to abolish religion, property, the nation-state, conventional notions of morality, and reality itself in the name of a new world.

Illuminati founder Adam Weishaupt was exposed and exiled but at that point his society had already infiltrated Masonic lodges in Europe where his subversive agenda would continue to operate in its inner porticos. Former President George Washington was warned that the Illuminati might have infiltrated his Masonic lodge in Alexandria, Virginia. In a letter published on the Library of Congress website, George Washington, responding to Reverend G. W. Snyder, wrote *I have heard much of the nefarious, and dangerous plan, and doctrines of the Illuminati, but never saw the Book until you were pleased to send it to me.*

The book that Snyder had sent to Washington, *Proofs of a Conspiracy,* authored by Scottish Professor of Natural Philosophy John Robison, 1797, *gives a full Account of a Society of Free-Masons, that distinguishes itself by the Name of 'Illuminati,' whose Plan is to overturn all Government and all Religion, even natural.* In his letter to Snyder, Washington concluded *I believe notwithstanding, that none of the Lodges in this Country are contaminated with the principles ascribed to the Society of the Illuminati.*

I agree with President Washington that American Freemasonry, which has been the primary network of secret societies in America since colonial times, was not seriously compromised by the Illuminati. While acknowledging that Freemasonry has played a positive and even to a degree a conservative role in American history and in the defining of American philosophy and culture, I would nevertheless note that Americans have a long and storied history of suspicion toward secret societies that require loyalty oaths and the Masonic Oath, which has been widely published, is troubling in its call for violence against those who violate it. I should note that the loyalty oath taken by high degree Masons leads me to believe that Masonry, which is no longer the most powerful secret network of secret societies in America, remains nevertheless a recruiting ground for the more powerful and identifiable network which is the infrastructure that broadly consists of the National Security Network.

President John F. Kennedy expressed this natural suspicion in a speech he delivered, a speech that is archived on the Kennedy Library website, on April 27, 1961, to the American Newspaper Publishers Association at their annual dinner at the Waldorf Astoria Hotel in New York City. President Kennedy stated the following:

The very word secrecy is repugnant in a free and open society; and we are as a people inherently and historically opposed to secret societies, to secret oaths and to secret proceedings. We decided long ago that the dangers of excessive and unwarranted concealment of pertinent facts far outweigh the dangers which are sited to justify it. Even today, there is little value in opposing the threat of a closed society by imitating its arbitrary restrictions. Even today, there is little value in ensuring the survival of our nation if our traditions do not survive with it. And there is very grave danger that an announced need for increased security will be seized upon by those anxious to expand its meaning to the very limits of official censorship and concealment. That I do not intend to permit to the extent that it is in my control. And no official of my Administration, whether his rank is high or low, civilian or military, should interpret my words here tonight as an excuse to censor the news, to stifle dissent, to cover up our mistakes or to withhold from the press and the public the facts they deserve to know.

Conservative social theory was expressed by Trump Administration chief strategist Steven K. Bannon who stated that the Trump administration was dedicated to the *deconstruction of the administrative state.* Conservative social theory holds that elected government officials are the constitutional authorities in terms of governing and passing laws. Indeed, this is the very essence of the democratic principle. We believe that our elected representatives, operating within the confines of a written constitution and balanced by chief executives, presidents, governors, mayors, and by a separate judicial branch, best represents and most accurately reflects our interests as citizens because elected officials conduct a limited public service within a prescribed period of time and within the confines of published and ratified constitutions and laws.

The administrative state involves a trend, going back to the early decades of the 20th Century, by which governing authority has been gradually transferred from elected officials to appointed and unaccountable bureaucracies. While we clearly benefit from a civil service that employs professionals who serve whichever administration is elected, as this has been an institution going back to the administration of President Rutherford B. Hayes, the unelected bureaucracy has nevertheless expanded and has exceeded it proper scope ever since assuming responsibilities previously held by elected officials.

The administrative state experienced major milestones after the 1912 election of Woodrow Wilson, America's first unabashedly socialist president. In his first year in office, Wilson presided over the passage of the 17th Amendment which resulted in the direct election of US Senators. This weakened the powers of state legislatures which had previously selected senators. The effect was stronger central government with senators more beholden to the Federal Government than to the states. That same year, the 16th Amendment was ratified which created the income tax and a permanent revenue collection agency, the Internal Revenue Service. The Federal Government would now know the personal business of every citizen and would get a direct cut of their income as opposed to raising revenue from apportionments from the states, tariffs on imports, and taxes and imposts on specific purchases at the time of the transaction. One of the lesser-known aspects of the 16th Amendment was the creation of tax advantaged non-profit corporations and foundations which would be used by the ruling class to park wealth into tax shelters, to employ family and friends, and to award groups with grants that supported their various political and social agendas.

Wilson signed the Federal Reserve Act on Christmas Eve, 1913, which transferred the power to create and to regulate the value of the American dollar from the US Treasury to a Federal Reserve System which is a consortium of private banks and investors. In 1919, Wilson signed the 18th Amendment into law which prohibited alcoholic beverages, and which constituted the first direct interference by the Federal Government into a social issue. Eight months after the Federal Reserve System was established, Europe devolved into the Great War. The United States would choose sides and enter into the war April of 1917. This was the true beginning of a policy by which the United States would become enmeshed into a world order, and this would include the trend by which America would begin to sacrifice national sovereignty and democratic principles to an informal world governing authority made up of unelected and unaccountable officials and bureaucracies.

In his Farewell Address, President George Washington established the guiding principle of American foreign policy which was to avoid foreign entanglements while extending a hand of friendship and peace to the nations of the world. This doctrine was expanded upon by President James Monroe in a doctrine that declared that America would protect the sovereignty of independent nations in the Americas against foreign attack and intrigue. World War I launched America into a new liberal doctrine, one that was described by historian Harry Elmer Barnes as *perpetual war for perpetual peace*. Wilson used the war as a means to try to create a new world order, as described by his chief foreign policy advisor Colonel Edward Mandell House, and as an excuse to create world government through the League of Nations. Domestically, Wilson used the war as an excuse to seize control over corporations, media, speech, elements of production and everyday life in a manner that reminds me of the Federal Government response to the COVID 19 pandemic.

In response to the 1929 Wall Street stock market crash which, according to University of Chicago economist Milton Freedman was precipitated by the Federal Reserve, and the subsequent economic depression, President Franklin D. Roosevelt declared a state of emergency, approved by Congress, in the form of bank holiday legislation. This effective suspension of the Constitution allowed the Roosevelt administration to advance the interests of what we now know as the administrative state. Using emergency powers, Roosevelt created a plethora of appointed and quasi-sovereign agencies such as the NRA, the CCC, the AAA, and other various agencies which came to be known as the alphabet agencies. These agencies assumed governing powers over many areas of American life, areas that had previously been regulated by congress, state and municipal elected officials, or powers that resided at the source of power, the self-regulating family and the citizen under God.

World War II led to a further internationalization of bureaucratic control as means to deal with the emergency. This caused a further transfer of governing authority from the sovereign American citizen into the hands of faceless and unaccountable bureaucracies. The entire structure, after the war, would veer in the direction of a growing international structure spearheaded by the United Nations. The aspiring rulers of the world would be in such interlocking groups as the World Trade Organization and would include a growing web of regional groups including the North American Treaty Organization and a lengthy list of Non-Governmental Organizations. I would argue that this modern internationalization of unelected and undemocratic governing power is traceable to Cecil Rhodes, the British imperial Governor of South Africa who, at the turn of the 20th Century, established secret societies as a means to launch world control under what has been described as an Anglo-American establishment.

While there would be numerous examples of the transfer of governing powers to the administrative state that could be sited, as the creation of the Department of Education and various environmental authorities come to mind, none would be more serious than that of the 1947 National Security Act which was signed into law by President Harry S. Truman. This act formalized an American secret infrastructure, an American interlocking series of secret societies which originally consisted of the Central Intelligence Agency and the National Security Council. This lead to the development of a massive and permanent secret network of complex and interlocking parts, public, quasi-public, private, all operating in the shadows of the law and many with their own black operational funding and international interface and outreach.

In retirement, President Truman wrote an editorial for the Washington Post, published December 22, 1963, entitled *Limit CIA Role to Intelligence*. In this revealing column, the contents of which were later echoed by President Dwight D. Eisenhower who warned America in his farewell address about the military-industrial complex, Truman warned America of the dangers associated with an emerging administrative state. Truman noted that the reason he agreed to create the CIA in the first place was simply as an intelligence gathering group that could consolidate the intelligence that was already being gathered by multiple existing agencies into a coherent and non-biased format for the president to review. President Truman wrote:

I decided to set up a special organization charged with the collection of all intelligence reports from every available source, and to have those reports reach me as President without department "treatment" or interpretations.

I wanted and needed the information in its "natural raw" state and in as comprehensive a volume as it was practical for me to make full use of it. But the most important thing about this move was to guard against the chance of intelligence being used to influence or to lead the President into unwise decisions – and I thought it was necessary that the President do his own thinking and evaluating.

President Truman concluded with statements that provide a leitmotif for conservative social theory and offer a guiding principle for all Americans: *But there are now some searching questions that need to be answered. I, therefore, would like to see the CIA be restored to its original assignment as the intelligence arm of the President, and that whatever else it can properly perform in that special field—and that its operational duties be terminated or properly used elsewhere.*

We have grown up as a nation, respected for our free institutions and for our ability to maintain a free and open society. There is something about the way the CIA has been functioning that is casting a shadow over our historic position, and I feel that we need to correct it.

The 2020 Election

Before vacating his office, Trump left behind one last lie, bigger than all the others, a tale of the worst betrayal of democracy in American history: the presidential election had been stolen. Hundreds of Republican elected officials broke their oaths in order to advance the lie, and 70 percent of Republican voters believed it, and this belief brought the year to its apocalyptic end two weeks before Inauguration Day, on January 6, when a mob that Trump had summoned to Washington and incited to march on Congress just as it was voting to ratify his opponent's victory — 20,000 neo-Confederate seditionists, QAnon conspiracists, white supremacists, and swag wearing Trumpists, with their hats and flags and face paint, their sagging bellies and jeans,- stormed the Capitol and looked for members of Congress to lynch, or else milled around taking selfies, while Trump watched with pleasure on TV, until our exhausted democracy mustered one last effort to save itself from destruction.

This passage from George Packer's book *Last Best Hope: America's crisis and renewal,* encapsulates the liberal view and narrative regarding the events that took place from November 3, 2020, Election Day, until January 6, 2021, the day Congress confirmed the election of Joe Biden and Kamala Harris as president and as vice president of the United States. I argue that these views reflect a narrative that is mostly false.

Firstly, Packer states that Trump lied when he stated that the election had been stolen. I would argue that this is a question that remains unresolved and that there is enough evidence available to suggest that Trump may have been right in his assertion. While this is a vast and complex topic that is beyond the scope of this book, I would suggest that a simple and objective examination by the reader of this issue, with a focus on the election as it unfolded in certain states, particularly Arizona, Georgia, Pennsylvania, Michigan, Wisconsin, Nevada and New Hampshire, would raise questions that might indicate significant election improprieties in those states and elsewhere. In order for us to examine this question fairly, we need to step away, at least briefly, from the mainstream media narrative, and we need to suspend our own bias and use sociological imagination as we do a bit of digging.

Packer goes on to assert, without providing any specifics, that *hundreds of Republican elected officials broke their oaths in order to advance the lie.* Since Packer does not site any evidence of any Republican official breaking his or her oath to the Constitution, nor does he name any names, we can therefore assume two lines of reasoning in order to approach what he might be implying with this outrageous allegation. Either Packer is suggesting that these hundreds of un-named Republican elected officials broke their respective oaths, assumedly to the Constitution, merely because they questioned the legitimacy of the election, which is their right and their responsibility both as elected officials and as citizens if they provide evidence to back their opinion, or he refers to those members of congress who formally requested that possible evidence in 7 states where the legitimacy of the Biden delegation was in question be heard at the ratifying assembly of January 6. Either way, those hundreds of Republican elected officials to which he refers, in fact, did not break their oath as they were operating not only entirely within the law and also within the constitutional traditions of our republic.

Packer notes that 70 percent of Republicans polled believed that the election had been stolen. He implies, falsely I would argue, that this belief was solely as a result of President Trump's assertion in this regard. The fact is that according to consistent polling over 70 percent of Republicans, and significant numbers of Democrats and Independents, did believe and continue to believe that the election was stolen. Those numbers have not changed much since shortly after election day. I would argue that the number of skeptics is probably a lot higher across the board as a percentage of those polled might feel too intimidated to answer the question honestly out of fear that their name might end up on a government list of "insurrectionists" or "terrorists" and that, as such, they might have to face consequences down the road.

Packer claims that Trump summoned a mob to Washington and had incited a march on Congress as they voted to ratify his opponents victory. Perhaps Packer could be given a bit of leeway here as evidence has emerged since he authored his book, putting aside witness testimony and video that has strangely been censored, that the ringleaders were FBI agents, Antifa dressed in Trump garb, Capitol police and various agents provocateurs. The march on the Capitol was led by Stuart Rhodes, head of the Oath Keepers, who evidence suggests was an FBI informant or agent and by John Sullivan, an affiliate of Antifa. Many of the ringleaders have not been charged with a crime but are considered to be un-indicted co-conspirators which may mean that they are protected agents. They are walking around while others who were merely on Capitol grounds are being held in a prison 9 months later without being formally charged with a crime. Reports are emerging from a prison in Washington where they are being detained in poor conditions including solitary confinement and beatings.

President Trump and many of his supporters, including myself on my own podcast, encouraged attendance at a peaceful protest rally as a means to show support for the congressional proceedings. There was a great deal of talk, in advance, of possible Antifa and even government infiltration by people who would try to cause trouble and engage in activities that would bring discredit to the peaceful rally that was planned. Trump spoke briefly at the mall where he called for peaceful protest while, unbeknownst to him, some people were marching on the Capitol where a handful of troublemakers broke in. The unprepared Capitol police put bicycle racks in as barriers, and some were filmed letting people into the building.

The day before the January 6 assembly, the FBI had obtained video footage of a man with a cell phone attempting to plant pipe bombs at the DNC and RNC Headquarters less than a block away from the Capitol. Yet, not much was done to secure a federal building that would contain most of the members of the US government at the same time. These facts raise some important questions regarding why the government did nothing to secure the Capitol in advance of this important meeting and whether or not the FBI had agents who knew in advance and who may have participated in the break-in. If this is the case, than what was their motive? We should not expect the partisan special congressional investigating committee to get to the bottom of any of this.

In order to place the January 6th assembly into proper context we should ask the age-old question that is always asked by investigators and that is *que bono* or who benefited. Clearly the Democratic Party, the Biden candidacy, and the elites who sought to confirm Biden as president were the sole beneficiaries of those infamous events at the Capitol. In order to understand how they benefited we should briefly review what was supposed to have transpired on January 6, 2021. In every presidential election year since 1798, both houses of Congress assemble on that day in order to confirm the presidential delegations that were ratified by each state for ratification. The candidate who receives 270 electoral votes wins the presidency. The Vice President of the United States is the president of this assembly. The vice president, as president of the assembly, has plenary powers to either recognize or to not recognize the respective state delegations.

Each state has a mechanism by which the delegation chosen by the state can be challenged if an alternative delegation contends that the election in their state had been unfairly certified. The challenge must be signed in a written note, signed by at least one congressman and by one senator. The signed note is delivered to the president of the assembly when the state is called, and the state is then granted up to 2 hours to present evidence of impropriety. This alleged evidence is openly debated by both sides. At the end of the allotted time, the president of the assembly then holds the plenary power to recognize one or the other of the delegations or to not recognize any delegation from that state. We should note that this procedure, entirely constitutional and, as such, completely within the purview of the oath to protect the Constitution, has been conducted during various assemblies going back to the election of 1800 when Vice President Thomas Jefferson, acting as president of the assembly, declared himself the winner in a contested race. More recently, Senator Barbara Boxer and Representative

Stephanie Tubbs Jones challenged the George W. Bush delegation from Ohio in the 2004 election.

Charges of election improprieties began to circulate on the night of the election and those charges continued to build momentum and evidence continued to emerge right up until the January 6th deadline for certification. Not only had the mainstream media refused to investigate any of this evidence, but instead the media employed the tactic of heaping scorn and vitriol upon anyone who did suggest impropriety. The scorn, divisive and insulting in nature, quickly devolved into outright censorship. As a result of the capitol incursion, Donald Trump, the sitting president of the United States, was censored and removed from his social platforms much to the consternation of many world leaders including Angela Merkel of Germany and Andres Manuel Lopez Obrador of Mexico. Many of those who examined the 2020 election in a manner that did not fit the mainstream narrative would subsequently also lose their social network platforms or would be shadow-banned.

Hundreds of eye-witness affidavits and over sixty lawsuits were filed across the country, all dismissed on technicalities. The evidence thus never made its way into a courtroom or into the media where it should have been heard and debated and where it should have been adjudicated upon. The general position of the judiciary across the board was that they did not want to intervene into a political matter. So much for an independent judiciary.

The January 6th assembly was the last opportunity for the evidence of voter impropriety to be heard and debated in public and in a constitutional setting. The media would have been forced to cover the proceedings live and the country would have at last had the opportunity to hear the evidence and we as a people would have then been free to make up our own minds. Just as the proceedings were getting under way, just as Arizona, called alphabetically, was beginning to present evidence of voter impropriety, the proverbial guy with his face-paint and his buffalo horns marched into the chamber and the proceedings were suspended. Then, later that day, around midnight, the assembly reconvened, with no media present, and gaveled Joe Biden and Kamala Harris into the presidency and vice presidency without any contests or hearings.

And so…I ask you dear reader…who benefited from the events of January 6th? Who was really responsible for a possible coup? The idea that this was an insurrection on the part of some hooligans is obviously absurd. How would a motley crew of unarmed and mostly peaceful nut-jobs be expected to overthrow the government? If anything, the insurrectionists were those who benefited from the suspension of the constitutional process of certification, a process that threatened to expose improprieties and call the anointing of the so-called winner into question. As it is, the narrative that this was an insurrection, and the false claim that Donald Trump intended to launch an insurrection, led to his second phony impeachment, completed after he left office, an event that wracked considerable damage to our cohesive social fabric and our democratic institutions. This final disgraceful impeachment was conducted with the false hope that such an event would politically wound Trump and the movement that he led while permanently diverting public attention away from the real and troubling series of events that surrounded the election itself.

George Packer finished this classic diatribe with ugly insults and derogatory descriptions of the appearance and the alleged actions of the ringleaders at the Capitol with the insinuation that, by doing so, he was describing President Trump and the fifty plus million people who voted for him. Packer hypocritically rails against political, economic and societal division while he stokes, and he creates the very division that he claims to be seeking to heal. Indeed, this division, this false dialectic is required by the social conflict theorists and the critical theorists, was false and phony from day one. Once we scratch the well-oiled surface, we, as Americans, will realize that while we naturally hold differences of opinion on real issues and while those differences might cause our emotions to boil over from time to time, we are nevertheless not really divided in terms of our love of country, of freedom, of unity, of preserving our individual interests and of advancing the institutions and ideas that support the same.

At least I would like to think so.

The Pandemic

The conservative approach to the COVID 19 pandemic, as illustrated by a social theory that considers individual responsibility as a paramount virtue, contributed toward a tendency to view government lockdowns as overreaction to what was clearly an international crisis. Conservatives instinctively guard against encroachments on civil and personal liberties. Conservatives viewed the mandates with a jaundiced eye and their suspicions were enhanced by self-serving over-reaching politicians. Those who tended to disagree with official positions on the pandemic, as dictated by establishment figures such as Dr. Anthony Fauci and other so-called experts, or who questioned the atmosphere of panic and fear that the mainstream media pushed, were denounced as anti-science or as conspiracy nuts. Legitimate opinions held by highly respected doctors and scientists, including many who were on the frontline of the pandemic, were routinely mocked and censored if those opinions deviated from the party line.

Conservatives tend to view questions of health as personal matters and they view the proper role of government in a health crisis to be, to quote President Theodore Roosevelt, that of the bully pulpit. We might obtain a more objective scientific picture of the proper response to the COVID 19 pandemic by conducting a brief examination of the response to the virus by Sweden. As a matter of public policy, Sweden approached the COVID 19 pandemic very differently than did the United States and many European countries. Sweden had no lockdowns, no mask requirements and no required social distancing as Swedish schools, businesses, restaurants, and institutions remained open.

Sweden allowed the virus to run its natural course while at the same time they inadequately protected their most vulnerable citizens. Sweden embraced the theory that herd immunity would develop under the assumption that a small percentage of the population might require hospitalization. The Swedish people continued on with their lives and went on with their business. The Swedish policy was described on their official website early in 2020: *rather than enforce a nationwide lockdown, the authorities have given recommendations: to stay home if you've got symptoms, to keep a distance to others, to avoid public transport, if possible, etc.* Sweden enforced mildly restrictive measures during specified surges such as limiting the number of people allowed into restaurants and gyms and testing for people entering the country. There were no masks and travel and tourism continued normally.

How did Sweden fare in terms of levels of contagion, hospitalization and death when compared to the United States and certain European nations which enforced restrictive policies? According to an article published by Reuters, Sweden's policy of keeping their schools open did not result in a higher rate of contagion amongst schoolchildren in Sweden when compared to schoolchildren in neighboring Finland which had closed their schools. Indeed, children made up an overall 2.1% of reported cases in Sweden during the period surveyed while in Finland, children made up 8.2%. Neither country reported deaths amongst children and severe cases were rare. Additionally, Sweden's Public Health Agency reported no increased risk for teachers regarding COVID 19 in comparison to other professions.

The mortality rate for COVID 19 patients that were admitted into intensive care units in Sweden during the first wave of the pandemic was lower than those recorded in other European countries and in the US states that reported high rates of contagion. Indeed, Sweden had an overall lower mortality rate in this period than did most European countries as well as the highly affected US States in 2020 Reuters reported that Sweden experienced a 7.7% increase in death rates from infectious diseases overall when compared to the previous 4 years while Belgium and Spain, which had extreme lockdowns, experienced an 18.1 and a 16.2% increases respectively.

Clearly Sweden suffered from COVID 19 as did other European countries and the United States, but Sweden responded by not locking down their country, by not closing their businesses and schools, and by not requiring their citizens to cover their faces. Evidence suggests that Sweden fared slightly better than did the nations that went into various degrees of lockdown. These facts might lead me to suggest that the lockdowns and most of the other restrictive mandates did not matter as the virus would take its toll either way.

During the pandemic, Swedish children continued to learn, Swedish small businesses stayed open, and life continued with relative normality. Sweden operated on a principle that we assumed represented the primary underlying principle of American society which was to confront a national crisis with local government responses and with personal responsibility and reasonable precaution. At the end of the day, the Swedish approach worked as well, if not slightly better, than did the authoritarian approach that was taken by certain American states and certain European nations.

An establishment view of American society during the pandemic was well expressed by journalist and author George Packer in his book *Last Best Hope* where he argues the following regarding the COVID-19 Pandemic:

*When the virus came here, it found a country with serious underlying
conditions, and it exploited them ruthlessly. Chronic ills—a corrupt political
class, a sclerotic bureaucracy, a heartless economy, a divided and distracted
public—had gone untreated for years. We learned to live, uncomfortably, with
the symptoms. It took the scale and intimacy of a pandemic to expose their
severity—to shock Americans with the recognition that we are in the high-risk
category.*

I would argue that it is not fair to argue that America had underlying conditions, per se, that impeded our ability to confront the COVID 19 pandemic. It appears that various nations that were dealing with the virus employed various approaches to the problem commensurate to what their respective cultures and experience would permit. To the degree that American society had such underlying conditions was the degree by which we forgot who we were as sovereign citizens under God. Perhaps we have become so welfare dependent, so morally corrupted by the dominant culture, and so imbued with the grievance inducing mindset that accompanies a culture based on critical theory that we were more willing to lay down in the face of state governors who became drunk with fiat power acting like little Mussolini's.

America's corrupt political class placed political obstacles in front of President Trump's reasonable and constitutional initial reaction to the virus, which was to ban travel from China which was, according to the WHO, the source of the virus. The response of the corrupt political class in this regard was to heap ridicule and scorn on Trump as a means to make hay against their political enemy. They set a pattern of putting politics over the lives of citizens as they engaged in such questionable agendas as discrediting the use of FDA approved drugs including Hydroxychloroquine and Ivermectin and even by discouraging such simple means of improving immunity as vitamin D and Zinc. While doctors who sought to prescribe those drugs were attacked as conspiracy theorists, governors in New York, Pennsylvania, Michigan and California were placing COVID 19 infected patients into nursing homes, a policy that I would describe as bordering on the genocidal.

New York governor Andrew Cuomo, who would be lionized by the corrupt political class as a great leader in the fight against COVID 19, and who received millions of dollars in advance for a book where he would chronicle his heroic leadership, ordered hospitals to send COVID 19 patients into nursing homes. As he did this, President Trump sent the Naval Hospital ship, with over a thousand beds and staffed with the nation's best military doctors and staff, to New York harbor for medical relief. The Naval Hospital sat in the harbor empty for five weeks because Cuomo thought that to use its facility might make Trump look good. Indeed, this irrational hatred of Trump, and this agenda to take him out of office, corrupted the entire response from top to bottom and led to blood on the hands of the conspirators.

George Packer, in his book *Last Best Hope: America in Crisis and Renewal* referred to a sclerotic bureaucracy. Sure! Demands were made on Trump by such figures as New York Mayor Wilhelm DeBlasio to declare martial law and call out the army. Perhaps if a more establishment figure than Trump had been president this would have been the result, martial law, military patrols to keep people locked down, a near equivalent to concentration camps for offenders and, in case you think I am exaggerating, this is exactly what happened in Australia after just a few cases of COVID 19. Liberal governors behaved like tin-horn dictators as they enacted draconian and contradictory dictates without state legislative approval. These types of dictates would be as diverse and illogical as Michigan Governor Gretchen Whitmer allowing people to purchase alcohol and lottery tickets but not garden seeds. More seriously, Democratic governors would use the pandemic as an excuse to circumvent the constitutional prerogative of their respective state legislatures by making election laws in violation of Article 2 of the US Constitution. Without legislative approval, these governors ordered the papering of their states with hundreds of thousands of unsolicited mail-in ballots in advance of the 2020 election.

George Packer refers to a heartless economy. Of course! Just like during the stock market crash of 1929, big business consolidated power and got filthy rich while mom and pop stores and small businesses went belly up due to the lockdowns. It seems that this could have been avoided if citizens were encouraged to take reasonable precautions to protect themselves against exposure to the virus, particularly our citizens who happen to be over eighty, or who have with pre-existing conditions, or who are obese. The lockdowns were indeed heartless, and, in addition, the long-term health, education and well-being of our children was ignored as we threw our children under the proverbial bus.

George Packer refers to a divided and distracted public, I blame the corrupt political class and their media lackeys for a deliberate and conscious agenda of division as they placed their agenda to take down Trump in an election year over the interests of the American people who faced the worst medical emergency in modern times. Certainly, President Trump is a flawed leader prone to mistakes. So was FDR during World War II. Trump was the president and, as such, in the interest of the country, the corrupt ruling elite should have put their agenda aside and, for the good of their fellow citizens and the country at large, they should have supported his efforts. They should have kept their critiques on a legitimate and fair plane instead of taking every opportunity to fan the flames of division.

As this book goes to press, Americans face draconian measures seeking to enforce vaccinations. To force a person to receive any medical procedure, let alone a needle injected into the arm, violates the spirit if not the letter of the Nuremburg Laws of post-World War II, laws that were meant to counter the heinous forced practices of Nazi doctors and psychiatrists, as well as American HIPPA laws. Laws are now being debated that would force children as young as four to get the vaccine in spite of the fact that Covid 19 is rare amongst children. There is a sense of distrust over whether reporting bad reactions to the vaccine, including amongst pregnant women and young men who have reported rare hart conditions, is being censored. These suspicions are enhanced by the fact that OSHA, responding to recent directives that are published on their website, no longer reports information or statistics regarding adverse reactions to the vaccine. I predict that liberal mothers will be at the vanguard in the fight against forced vaccines for children.

Americans are now concerned about electronic vaccine passports which, according to Senator Rand Paul, will lead to a total surveillance state and will expand government power and suppress liberty worldwide. The World Economic Forum launched the Great Reset Initiative in June 2020, in response to a pandemic that they viewed as more than a mere disease. They viewed the crisis as an opportunity to advance their vision to create an informal and a mostly privately oriented and controlled new world order.

These are the descendants of the so-called benevolent dictators who hatched both Nazism and Communism, the two progressive movements that sought the same goals in the context of their times. The agenda remains a step-by-step ending of private property, national sovereignty, and the rights of the individual under God.

Collective Effervescence

French Sociologist Emile Durkheim identified the social concept of Collective Effervescence. Along with Max Weber and Karl Marx, Durkheim is viewed as one of the founders of Sociology and as the primary organizer of Structural Functionalism which remains one the main schools of sociological thought today. Structural Functionalism seeks to maintain the intricate web of social institutions that constitute society within a rational context of reform and modernization based on the attainment of scientific knowledge. Durkheim believed in social change as a means toward social improvement based on moral and ethical understanding and on the identification of truths as opposed to change for the sake of change.

Collective effervescence is a natural phenomenon, one that is required in order for individuals and for societies to organize and function. As individuals, we engage in degrees of collective effervescence in order to conduct both professional and personal relationships. The classic example of collective effervescence would be the marriage relationship by which the traditional marriage relationship might overlook certain negative things about the other, to turn a blind eye so to speak, in order to preserve an equilibrium and advance the more important elements of the relationship. In the micro sense, collective effervescence serves as the means by which we have a good relationship with each other.

Durkheim studied how to improve institutions and societies as a whole by means of understanding the natural, or as he stated, the organic elements that held society together, and to then separate out that which is true in terms of that which best serves the interests of the sovereign individual, and that which is false and, as such, that which retards those interests. In this way, Durkheim differed from Marx and Weber who, as conflict theorists, were interested in societal divisions and who sought to isolate and then exploit those divisions as a means to tear down societies, and in the broad sense to tear down reality, so as to create the new man and the new society which would then be molded in their so-called enlightened image.

Collective effervescence describes group experience that involves a heightening of consciousness by those participating. Durkheim viewed this experience as involving religion and he wrote about the totem which is a sociological term that describes either a physical object or a specific ritual that would become a locus of the experience. The definition of collective effervescence has expanded to include various public events that are experienced collectively by participants such as a baseball game, a rock concert, a theatre performance or a political rally. The totem becomes the team, the rock band, the performance, the politician. When we attend such events, we briefly become part of a collective experience that is enhanced by timing and by a general willingness to temporarily suspend degrees of our own consciousness so as to take in the experience. In such circumstances, we open ourselves up to passively receive information either for the sake of edification or for the sake of entertainment.

Collective effervescence is a natural force that can be harnessed for good, benign, or bad purposes. Collective effervescence in the service of outrage over injustice or evil, as a force to harness positive action for change, is a force for good because in those cases it resonates with and advances truths. In the broad sense governments promote collective effervescence on a mass and subtle scale as means to advance agendas both positive and negative. The method that government employs in this regard is known as propaganda. This same method is employed by an advertising or a marketing agency, or by a public relations firm as means to promote a brand of automobile or a brand of tooth paste.

Governments use propaganda as a means to create an atmosphere of collective effervescence so as to prepare a population to go to war, accept a tax increase, or to accept restrictions in the face of a perceived or real national emergency such as a pandemic. This preparation, for better or worse, involves a level of control by the government, either formal or informal, over the media or, as Marx described it in *The Communist Manifesto*, control over the *means of communication*. As would be the case with marketing a product or a service, there are levels of deception associated with a propaganda campaign, a tendency to embellish the positive while downplaying or omitting the bad, and there is a line that can be crossed in terms of what would be considered the difference between normal boosterism and outright lying. Indeed, the purpose of a free media, as codified in the first amendment of the Constitution, is to investigate and to ferret out truth from falsehood and analyze areas in between that might be subject to interpretation.

The Nazis advanced propaganda and the creation of an enhanced, radicalized and weaponized form of collective effervescence. They did this by brilliantly manipulating and coordinating collective experience to the point where the participants would become almost completely submissive and would become as close as humanly possible to falling into a hypnotic state of mental submission. Examples of this tactic in action, as recorded by Nazi documentary filmmaker Leni Riefenstahl, were the mass rallies held to promote Hitler. Those rallies, held at night as a means to enhance the effect and to reduce external stimuli would include bonfires which would enhance sight and smell, booming loudspeakers and media devices and visuals including movies, symphonies, huge flags, bright colors, and Nazi symbols meant to stir emotions.

With storm-troopers goose-stepping in precise formation, with shiny boots and sharp uniforms, Richard Wagner's Flight of the Valkyries blaring on loudspeakers, standards hoisted high, gigantic flags and bunting, strobe-lights and smoke from bonfires, by rabble-rousing speeches, Hitler would solemnly and triumphantly mount the stage and begin speaking in almost a whisper, then he would slowly begin to raise his voice with rage and with expressions twisted with hate he would begin to gesticulate with well-practiced and increasingly violent gestures until he reach a crescendo of screams, cries and orgasmic shaking of his arms and body. There were reports of women fainting in the audience and having orgasms. I would suggest that various politicians and organized groups have since then learned from the Nazis, and they have imitated their tactics in more refined forms.

Sociology defines mass hysteria as phenomena that results from the spreading of an illusion of threats and an impending sense of doom, whether real or imaginary. These illusions, rumors, fears, when properly executed, might spread through a population like a knife through butter. Examples of this type of fear-mongering, in milder and more localized forms, happens all the time as a person or a group might find themselves ostracized, shunned, exiled or worse due to lies and exaggerations that were quietly spread by a person, or by a group that was motivated by hate, greed or envy. The rumor-mongers might be themselves plagued by fears or by ignorance or they might be innocently reacting to earlier rumors. Governments might be motivated to endorse or promote such rumors, and stoke fears, against an enemy during war in order to portray the enemy in exaggerated and demonized terms while keeping the war-weary population onboard. Motives for creating or exacerbating mass hysteria are numerous and are unique to a particular situation.

A classic example of mass hysteria in America was the Salem witch trials of 1692-1693. Mass hysteria on a social level is more often than not sustained when rumors and fears receive either explicit or implicit support from governments as was the case with the Salem hysteria which may have petered out had local governments not sided with the accusers and stood by while courts issued convictions. Peasant revolts in Europe, particularly the Great Fear that preceded the French Revolution, often involved false conspiracy theories that were stoked by rival princes and secret societies that were seeking to stir people up with accusations against perceived enemies.

I suggest that the social phenomena that is the anti-Trump movement is a broad example of mass hysteria. Certainly, the usual suspects, the American far left, are at the core of this phenomena. They have traditionally sought to undermine American society by destroying their opposition with brutal attacks and scorched earth. Yet they have operated on the fringes of American life as have their far-right counterparts. Americans have traditionally spurned such approaches. Yet, the opposition to President Trump has been somehow different. There is something twisted, something emotional and irrational at its core, something bizarre and inexplicable seems to be going on. Perhaps this reflects the possibility that elements of the anti-American far-left have finally gone mainstream. Americans have often disagreed on public policy questions and issues of culture and style, and at times those disagreements have reached a boiling point but…with Trump…there was no particular issue that might have triggered this mass hysteria, nothing beyond the usual menu of normal differences and grievances, those that usually exist between liberals and conservatives.

I suggest that the reaction to the election of Donald Trump as President of the United States by elements of the opposition has not been normal to America. The day after Election Day, 2016, I was broadcasting at Tufts University, and I observed how the College offered students *safe spaces* to help them come to grips with the election. College students at one of America's most prestigious universities were sitting on the floor with playdough and toys. On a day when all Americans, from all sides of the political spectrum have traditionally celebrated the most glorious institution of the American Republic, the peaceful and orderly transfer of power to a new administration, privileged Tufts students felt so traumatized or gripped with rage and hate that they were afraid of their own shadows. This ridiculous situation did not happen by accident.

I can recount terrible experiences that I personally, as an open supporter of President Trump, had to endure and terrible things that I witnessed at the time, and I am sure that other open supporters of Trump can recount similar experiences. I will mention one small and insignificant example before moving on. I was told in advance that the Thanksgiving dinner that I was invited to attend that year was to be a "Trump free zone." I remember the scowls and ashen faces around the table as I quietly sipped my wine and scarfed down the turkey and trimmings.

From the standpoint of social theory, the anti-Trump hysteria breaks down into two camps, the witting and the unwitting. The witting and fully conscious camp of anti-Trumpers were mostly well-heeled internationalists and elitists, both Democrat and Republican, those who were accurately described by Occupy Wall Street as the top one percent. In fact, the very core of this camp consisted of most of the major players on Wall Street. This group, which includes American and some foreign elitists, fears and loathes Trump because Trump is a nationalist who articulates his intention to put America first. For Trump, unlike his recent predecessors who mouthed this idea as a bumper-sticker slogan to fool people to get elected, the idea of putting America first was his true intention. While they claimed that Trump was a liar, they privately feared him because he spoke truths on things that mattered.

They were afraid that Trump might wake up the sleeping giant. The American people might become aware of who they are and become conscious of their own agency as sovereign citizens living in an independent republic founded on democratic principles. This possibility threatens everything they have been building for the past hundred years. Trump threatened to bring down the whole rotten house of cards and Trump meant business when he spoke of draining the swamp and taking on the deep state. Trump summed up the meaning of his presidency when he stated, in his inaugural address: *today we are not merely transferring power from one administration to another, or from one party to another, but we are transferring power from Washington, D.C., and giving it back to you, the people.*

The fully witting camp of Trump haters engaged in a conspiracy that sought to remove Trump from office or to at least hobble his presidency and, by proxy, the movement that he led as much as possible. This group, operating within the very deep state that Trump sought to reform and reign in, included former Director of National Intelligence James Clapper, former CIA Director John Brennan, former FBI Director Robert Mueller, fired FBI Director James Comey, possibly Comey's successor at the FBI Christopher Wray, former Assistant FBI Director Andrew McCabe, FBI agent Peter Strzok and his lover FBI Attorney Lisa Page among an elaborate and byzantine web of others fanning across other branches of government.

The clandestine activities of this group, which is much larger than the few principle players named here, is a fascinating topic that is beyond the focus of this book about social theory. Suffice to say that these fully witting Trump haters meant business, they spied on Trump, they distributed a phony dossier, they used spies overseas, they set up small players like Carter Page and George Papadopoulos and they tampered with evidence. They were able to get in place a special prosecutor, Robert Mueller, who then spent millions going after people who had little or nothing to do with anything relevant while promoting a preposterous conspiracy theory claiming that Trump was spying for Russia. They eventually impeached the duly elected president twice on completely bogus charges.

Other fully witting participants in this conspiracy would include media figures such as Rachel Maddow at MSNBC, Jeff Zucker at CNN, Mark Zuckerberg at Facebook, Jack Dorsey at Twitter, and others who fanned out at the top of big media and big tech. These people did the bidding of the conspirators by promoting, by means of the drip…drip…drip method, a method which is analogous to Chinese water torture, both what Trump accurately called fake news, and by an extremely negative attack on Trump policies and actions while obscuring and ignoring positive news. One example of this daily digest of negative propaganda, dished out by most of the major networks, the big city newspapers, big tech, and a network of regional and local sycophants, was the story, given massive coverage, that Trump had asked a waiter at a state dinner for an extra scoop of vanilla ice cream on his pie. We were to somehow, subconsciously, made to think that this was bad.

The second camp of those afflicted with this abnormal Trump derangement, what I describe as a form of mass hysteria, is the half-witting average American. About a week after the election, I was at a high-school debate event where I served as a parent judge. In the parents lounge, two mothers were having a melt-down over the election of Trump. These two otherwise respectable mothers, both well to do suburban women, were shaking with rage as they simultaneously babbled incoherently about the bad orange man. I believe that they, along with the rest of the millions of well-meaning and sober liberals around the country similarly afflicted, have been the victim of what I would loosely describe as a massive campaign of brainwashing.

As mentioned earlier, the Nazis had mastered the art and science of mass propaganda as a means of creating a form of mass hypnosis, an enhancement, a weaponizing, a gain of function if you will, of Durkheim's collective effervescence. This research continued after the war with the CIA's MKUltra project, with Britain's Tavistock Institute and with the Soviet Union's psychological research. Enough about this is now publicly known, partially due to the de-classification that accompanied the Church Committee hearings of the late 1970's, for me to state that I am not engaging here in a conspiracy theory. Indeed, this is a fascinating subject that I would suggest that you, dear reader, dig into on your own. Suffice to say that elements within our government, elements that were part of the formal secret society that President Trump accurately referred to as the deep state, picked up the Nazi thread and continued to experiment with methods of both individual and mass mind control. It appears to me that the mass hysteria against Trump is part of that experimentation carried out on a mass scale.

Those who sought to promote this mild form of mass hysteria, in a manner classic to the left, sought to exploit genuine societal problems for their own gain. In the case of Trump, the difference between this conventional approach by the left, an approach that goes back to the days of the French Revolution, is that the accusations against Trump and his followers were a complete and utter lie. The core of that accusation is that Donald Trump and, by proxy, his movement, secretly have something against black men and women. This lie then branches off into a more general and elaborate thesis which is that Trump and his movement have something against everyone other than white Christian heterosexual men.

Emanating out of the critical theory which sought to divide American society with the preposterous claim that middle class Americans were unconscious fascists, the anti-Trump critical theorists divided America on the aforementioned lines. The conscious conspirators deliberately fanned the flames of division for self-serving reasons which was to get rid of the nationalist leader and to destroy a nationalist movement that genuinely sought to empower all Americans from all backgrounds. They sought to keep Americans, particularly minorities, in a state of either mild somnambulance or agitation based on their exploitation of genuine grievance. Minorities, inundated by conspiratorial lies, would thus be expected to disregard their own interests as citizens and as Americans.

This was why a corrupted establishment, one that has at this point become completely shot through with Trump derangement, removed Trump from office. This was why that had to drive a wedge between the movement that Trump led and its natural constituency, people of color and millennials. This was why establishment players such as Mark Zuckerberg, one of the richest men in history, and his wife shelled out 420 million dollars out of their own pockets to two organizations could hand out walking around money to thousands of activist poll workers and absentee ballot counters in certain states in advance of the 2020 election. This was why billionaire George Soros financed the election of activist secretaries of states, district attorneys and sheriffs who would control election precincts. This was why voting machines all shut down simultaneously in select states on election eve, at a moment when Trump was ahead in all cases, leading those states to stop counting. Those same states would then re-open and resume counting hours later with Biden suddenly and inexplicably ahead.

Transhumanism

The social-scientific movement that is now known as Transhumanism originated in the mid-19th Century with the 1859 publication of Charles Darwin's world-famous book *On the Origin of Species by Means of Natural Selection or the Preservation of Favored Races in the Struggle for Life*. This book contained *Darwin's* theory of evolution which suggests that all of life had somehow sprung out of the crashing together of non-living matter. Darwin, borrowing from German enlightenment philosopher Georg Hegel, viewed biological life as evolving due to a dialectical process which he believed was the cause of biological progress and specie differentiation. By means of natural selection, superior members of a species would have sex with other superior members thus giving birth to more superior offspring.

By this means, the more fit members of the species would survive, thrive, and gradually advance through what Darwin suggested was a process of survival until, after umpteen millions of years, out would pop a new and superior species with advanced features. Meanwhile, the weaker, or the more inferior members of the species would gradually fall by the wayside and die out or they would be annihilated. Darwin was also influenced by British economist Thomas Malthus, author of *An Essay on the Principle of Population*. Malthus proposed a theory of scarcity writing: *The power of population is indefinitely greater than the power in the earth to produce subsistence for man.*

Transhumanism continues onward in a quest toward the evolution of mankind, or at least the evolution of an elite segment of mankind as the next rung in the evolutionary chain, a new and superior species, or a new and superior race as Darwin described it. This new, superior, more evolved species, or race of man would, according to Transhumanism, include both biological and technological components. Transhumanism continues in the philosophical vein of Francis Galton, Darwin's cousin and collaborator, who coined the term eugenics which derives from the Greek word for better birth. Galton wanted to speed up the process of natural selection so mankind would not have to wait umpteen millions of years for a new species of human being to emerge. The scientifically minded Galton advocated state-sponsored breeding for the same reason that Malthus advocated state-sponsored control of food production for population control.

Conservative social theory is supportive of ethical scientific research that contributes to the improvement and advancement of human life. In this regard, it should be acknowledged that aspects of the research attendant to Transhumanism and to similar fields including artificial intelligence may potentially yield certain positive results. An example of such positive research was conducted by futurist Ray Kurzweil who is viewed as one of the founders of modern Transhumanism. Kurzweil invented the Talking Book in the 1980's which translated written pages into audio sound. Kurzweil invented this incredible device for Stevie Wonder. When asked if he believes in God, Kurzweil responded: Does God exist? I would say…not yet.

Ray Kurzweil wrote about life extension which he views as a step toward the ultimate emergence of a new species of human being which would contain implanted computer components and chips. These computer components and chips, which should be viewed in the context of the *internet of things*, would monitor various aspects of a person's health and would theoretically make available to the person millions of bits of information. The end result, according to Kurzweil and his followers would be a new human being who would have the equivalent of cosmic consciousness, who would live for as long as two centuries in good health and who would have a beautiful appearance. This vision reminds me of the analogous vision of the Nazi Ubermench, which was that of the blond haired, blue-eyed Aryan who had super strength, who would live for centuries and who would possess cosmic consciousness.

The modern religion of Transhumanism, and make no mistake, Transhumanism is a religion, while tracing back to ancient pagan cults that worshipped man-made images, was developed in modern times by, among others, Russian aristocrat and mystic Helena Petrovna Blavatsky. In 1875, Blavatsky co-founded the Theosophical Society in New York City, a society that influences the United Nations where it maintains a meditation room. Theosophy seeks a merge between Darwin's Theory of Evolution, occultic beliefs and science. Theosophy does not believe in the one God as the giver of moral and ethical law. Theosophy believes that evolution will lead to a final utopian stage where a select group of men and women will become gods.

British fiction writer Aldus Huxley, grandson of T. H. Huxley who was the primary promoter of Darwin's theory of evolution at the time of the publication of Darwin's book authored *Brave New World* in 1931. This influential book presents a futuristic world government drawn on scientific lines similar to the theosophic vision. Huxley wrote of an environmentally engineered society employing psychological manipulation, conditioning, and various scientific advances creating a hermetically sealed world. Huxley committed suicide by LSD, a suicide that he filmed, one that was eclipsed in publicity by the assassination of President John F. Kennedy which occurred the same day, November 22, 1963. Shortly before his death, the author of the 1951 autobiographical book *The Doors of Perception* wrote of a world where everyone would be hooked on a pharmaceutical drug and would exist in a medically induced and informal world concentration camp.

Joe Allen is a blogger and a contributor to Stephen K. Bannon's War Room Pandemic podcast. An expert on Transhumanism, Allen writes on the emergence of what he refers to as an international tyranny that is finding its footing in response to the COVID 19 pandemic. He notes that several pilot programs were launched including one in 2018 by Swedish company Biohax International which injected chips into the palms of over 4,000 Swedes which included a radio frequency identification devise (RFID), each the size of a grain of rice. This experiment was reported on by the *National Public Radio* broadcast *All Things Considered*, October 22, 2018, and published in an article on the NPR website entitled *Thousands of Swedes are inserting microchips under their skin*, by the *British Independent* in an October 26, 2018, article entitled *Swedish Cyborg Craze sees more than 4,000 Swedes insert chips under their skin*, and also on January 3, 2018, by *Ars Technica, A Practical Guide to Microchip Implants*.

The Biohax implant offers the recipient access to the workplace, home and elsewhere while monitoring health and keeping records of cashless transactions. A Seattle based bio implant company, Dangerous Things, estimates that 50-100 thousand people are chipped around the world by various tech companies. The scholarly journal *Science Transnational Medicine* published *Biocompatible near infrared quantum delivered to the skin by microneedle patches record vaccination* which focuses on the quantum dot tattoo. With research by a group of MIT scientists funded by Bill Gates, the quantum dot tattoo is administered with a microneedle into the skin where it can be scanned by a specially modified smartphone. Lab mice experiments indicate that the quantum dot tattoo might last for up to five years and the project's leader, quoted in the *Science Transnational Medicine* article, stated that the goal is for the tattoo to reach a level of *widespread adoption* in humans. These technologies are part of a growing field known as the *Internet of Bodies* a physiological version of the *Internet of Things* and the technology has been discussed at the World Economic Forum in Davos, Switzerland.

Xaio Liu is an assistant professor at McGill University and a Fellow at the Centre for the Fourth Industrial Revolution which is part of the World Economic Forum. In an article published by the World Economic Forum, June 4, 2020, entitled *Tracking how our bodies work could change our lives*, Dr. Xaio advocates the use of bio sensors to monitor both personal as well as public health. In this article, Dr. Xaio writes that the bio sensors would be in the form of a Fit Bit, which could be implanted, or swallowed in pill form. Joe Allen notes that these devices which monitor and chronicle bodily functioning, could be connected to a wider digital environment.

German professor and economist Klaus Schwab is the founder and Executive Chairman of the World Economic Forum. Joe Allen reports that in 2016 Schwab was asked when humans might be implanted with digital brain chips. He responded: *Certainly, in the next ten years. And at first, we will implant them in our clothes. And then we could imagine that we will implant them in our brains, or in our skin. And in the end, maybe, there will be a direct communication between our brain and the digital world. What we see is a kind of fusion of the physical, digital, and biological world.*

Transhumanism requires both overt and covert use of force for its enactment as this vision would lead to an end of property, sovereignty, faith, family, individual freedom and an end to the independently functioning brain. Indeed, this form of electronic enslavement, which is the modern embodiment of a socialistic vision of human society, a vision that goes back, metaphorically, to the fall in the Garden of Eden and to Nimrod's Tower of Babel, which was an attempt to reach into heaven and overthrow God, would put an end to the independent human being. As mentioned, this is not to dismiss certain genuinely positive medical advances that might emerge from this research but, in the hands of the transhumanists, such research would be used to end life as we know it.

Such a development as described by the transhumanists would require for implementation a perceived condition of emergency, one that would generate such fear in the populace that the nations and peoples of the world would surrender their freedom in order to save themselves. The 20th Century witnessed such emergencies which were exploited if not outright manufactured by the same ruling elites as constitute todays transhumanists. In the 20th Century, those conditions of emergency included two World Wars, forced famines, economic depressions and, more recently, world terrorism. Indeed, the Carnegie Endowment for International Peace, according to testimony from the Reece Committee hearings of the 1950's, held sessions over a year to try to figure out how to bring about world socialism. Their answer was to instigate a world war, and this is exactly what happened in 1914, a few years after the end of their secretive deliberations.

The Report from Iron Mountain, published in 1967, was authored by a Special Study Group of fifteen men headed by Harvard professor and economist John Kenneth Galbraith. While the report has been called a spoof, nevertheless this report has a ring of authenticity on a number of issues. In a manner similar to the earlier Carnegie Foundation report, the Iron Mountain report concluded that perpetual war was the best policy toward centralizing governments and drawing nations closer, as part of a stage in a dialectical process, toward the development of informal world government. Iron Mountain proposed two scenarios that might, with proper media coordination, contribute toward the needed atmosphere of fear and a required sense of impending emergency. Those two proposals were the promotion of impending environmental catastrophe that might lead to human extinction and a pending invasion of the world from flying saucers carrying aliens from outer space.

The World Economic Forum is only the most recent permutation in a long line of modern secret societies, going back to the Bavarian Illuminati of Adam Weishaupt, that seeks to establish a world run by a self-appointed managerial elite. The WEF consists of an unholy alliance between governments, private multi-national corporations with assets of no less than $5 billion and select non-governmental organizations. They seek informal control over the politics, economy, culture and religions of the world. Their annual conference in Davos, Switzerland attracts world political leaders, economists, billionaires and cultural and religious movers and shakers.

In a 2015 article in *Foreign Affairs*, published by the Council on Foreign Relations, a secretive group that promotes perpetual war and that has counted amongst its members most American Secretaries of States starting in the 1940's, Klaus Schwab, founder and Chairman of the World Economic Forum unveiled what he called the Fourth Industrial Revolution as involving the global coordination of technologies including hardware, software, biology, and means of electronic communication. At Davos, 2017, Schwab described this revolution as including *The possibilities of billions of people connected by mobile devices, with unprecedented processing power, storage capacity, and access to knowledge, are unlimited. And these possibilities will be multiplied by emerging technology breakthroughs in fields such as artificial intelligence, robotics, the Internet of Things, autonomous vehicles, 3-D printing, nanotechnology, biotechnology, materials science, energy storage, and quantum computing.*

In his book *COVID 19: The Great Reset*, Klaus Schwab called for a reset in response to the COVID 19 pandemic, one that would reset our global social, economic and political systems from the ground up. This is classic Conflict Theory which calls for change by tearing down that which exists and, by a dialectical process, initiating a new synthesis. In the view of Karl Marx, who's principles guide the Conflict Theory sociological school of thought, the new synthesis would be Communism, a world of absolute equality where old prejudices that make us unequal including property, sovereignty, and the independent mind are replaced by automatons living in harmony with nature in a manner comparable to ants who build elaborate underground colonies.

The socio-political vision of Klaus Schwab and the World Economic Forum is less ambitious when compared to Conflict Theory. The WEF embraces a socio-political theory that was coined in the early 20th Century, one that is known as Convergence. In practice, this theory would have involved the convergence of the Soviet Union, which would theoretically move to the right, and the United States would theoretically move to the left. Both nations would reach a point of convergence where both would be in a joint position to informally govern a world system containing elements of both communism and capitalism. H. Rowan Gaither, president of the Ford Foundation, testifying to Norman Dodd, staff director of the 1954 Reese Committee hearings, which was a congressional hearings charged with investigating the influence of foundations on American politics and culture, described this policy.

Of course, you know that we at the executive level here were, at one time or another, active in either the O.S.S., the State Department, or the European Economic Administration. During those times, and without exception, we operated under directives issued by the White House. We are continuing to be guided by just such directives…. The substance [of these directives] was to the effect that we should make every effort to so alter life in the United States as to make possible a comfortable merger with the Soviet Union.

The WEF, as evidenced by their website lays open their agenda in no uncertain terms, embraces an update in convergence except, this time around, they seek to use emerging technologies that would eventually transfer governing powers to a world entity that would be something other than human. They operate out of a sense of weakness. They lack the confidence of past world order leaders such as Adolf Hitler, Josef Stalin, and the massive international kleptocracy of socialistic secret societies and elites who promoted their respective open agendas by fanning out across the globe and subverting freedom-oriented institutions while conspiring to corrupt freedom-oriented ideas.

These same elites seem to finally understand that the sovereign human being, under God, cannot be subdued by the naked force of the man-made state or by subversive and deceptive action. The ruling elites have had their great moments of success and they will no doubt keep trucking along. They had their Holocausts, their genocides, democides, induced famines, economic depressions, their pandemics and their terror campaigns. The human spirit rises up, wipes the proverbial blood from the face, and meets evil in the field of battle where they are restrained and outright defeat by exposure and the identification of their satanic agenda. This leads to disintegration and collapse on top of lies, contradictions, and massive spider-like webs of deceit. This is why they are now seeking to transfer power to inanimate objects that they hope they can electronically program for eternity. This is also why the crisis that we now face today is even more dangerous and even more potentially deadly than any that the permanent conspiracy has ever dished up to us freedom loving citizens previously. They will lose in the end but at what cost?

Conclusion

I paradoxically argue that conservatism is an anti-ideology. Conservative social theory is not an ideology cooked up out of thin air. I contrast conservatism with ideologies that are invented as abstract realities that emanate out of the fecund and biased imaginations of imperfect and overly ambitious minds. I contend that conservatism involves the practical individual and society attempting to establish and build upon the best elements of that which is real and that which is right. Conservative theory serves as a foundation upon which the individual might improve and advance their own individual life within the context of a society and a nation that preserves, protects and defends the natural rights of all of its citizens to life, liberty and the pursuit of happiness.

This brief book is my humble presentation of an American conservative social theory, one that is based upon American ideals and American philosophy. I am inspired by those ideals not only because I am an American and I unabashedly hold a conscious bias toward my own country, but also because I also happen to believe that fundamental aspects of those American ideals that I hold so dear are universal. I believe in those ideals and principles because they are true and right, might hopefully inspire other individuals or societies within the context of their own sovereign interests and unique culture and lifestyle.

I shall conclude this conservative social theory with a brief examination of *The 1776 Report* which was published on January 18, 2021, two days before President Donald J. Trump left office. President Trump established the *President's Advisory 1776 Commission* on October 6, 2020, the purpose of which was to create a blueprint for patriotic education and as a means to counter the growing and insidious influence of Critical Race Theory which had been rolled out a year earlier by the New York Times as *The 1619 Project*. The 1776 Commission would be disbanded by President Joseph R. Biden in his first day in office following a coordinated smear campaign that had been launched against it.

Trump's executive order establishing the 1776 Commission offers a clear expression of traditional American social philosophy. The executive order called for *a rising generation to understand the history and principles of the founding of the United States in 1776 and, through this, form a more perfect union. The American founding envisioned a political order in harmony with the design of "the Laws of Nature and of Nature's God," seeing the rights to life, liberty, and the pursuit of happiness as embodied in and sanctioned by natural law and its traditions.*

The United States was established as an exceptional nation. *The formation of a republic around these principles marked a clear departure from previous forms of government, securing rights through a form of government that derives its legitimate power from the consent of the governed.* With few exceptions, other nations and other societies, from ancient times until the founding of the American Republic, claimed that rights emanated from a dictator who would grant subjects privileges as favors that suited his arbitrary whim. The dictator would claim, in variations hovering between overt and subtle, that his legitimacy came from God. In America, the government would derive its legitimacy not from God but rather from the consent of the governed and the citizen, not the dictator, would be endowed by God with inalienable rights.

The American founding envisioned a political order in harmony with the design of "the Laws of Nature and of Nature's God," seeing the rights to life, liberty, and the pursuit of happiness as embodied in and sanctioned by natural law and its traditions.

The formation of a republic around these principles marked a clear departure from previous forms of government, securing rights through a form of government that derives its legitimate power from the consent of the governed.

With few exceptions, governments from ancient times until the founding of the American Republic claimed that rights emanated from a dictator who granted favors that suited arbitrary whim. The dictator claimed that his governing legitimacy emanated from God. The American form of government would derive legitimacy not from God but rather from the consent of the governed. The American citizen, not a dictator, would be endowed by God with certain inalienable rights. This core conservative principle makes America exceptional because this most principle reflects that which is true and that which is most efficacious to human advancement. Indeed, this idea resides at the very core of what makes America progressive in the true sense.

Against this history, in recent years, a series of polemics grounded in poor scholarship has vilified our Founders and our founding. Despite the virtues and accomplishments of this Nation, many students are now taught in school to hate their own country, and to believe that the men and women who built it were not heroes, but rather villains. This radicalized view of American history lacks perspective, obscures virtues, twists motives, ignores or distorts facts, and magnifies flaws, resulting in the truth being concealed and history disfigured. Failing to identify, challenge, and correct this distorted perspective could fray and ultimately erase the bonds that knit our country and culture together.

Conservative social theory, based upon the principles of sociologist Emil Durkheim's idea of systematic functionalism, views American history and culture as a glass half full and not as a glass half empty. Conservative social theory seeks to reform and improve social institutions that edify society so as to make them more reflective of the better interests of society. When the American Republic was founded on July 4, 1776, for the first time in human history the citizen was recognized as sovereign and government was recognized as an instrument, subservient to the sovereignty of the citizen, that was to be a vehicle to preserve, protect and defend individual sovereignty which came from the creator.

While the critical theorists quite accurately note that this enfranchisement of sovereign citizen power in 1776 was exclusive to white male landowners, they miss the point when they ignore the fact that such enfranchisement did not exist at all for any group, other than the dictator and his immediate retinue, anywhere else in the world at that time, that this enfranchisement had never existed before at any time or anywhere else in history. They also failed to notice that at the time of the American Revolution, several states had already abolished slavery and that those states were the first governments in history to do so.

Indeed, the founding of the American Republic got the ball rolling in terms of enfranchising more people over time. This progression of individual rights is in accord with conservative social theory which views every life as unique, as crafted in the image of God and, as such, as equal in the eyes of God. American society would, as motivated by these powerful and, dare I suggest, revolutionary forces when viewed in the context of the world system, has moved its citizenry forward ever since in terms of enfranchisement. After a bloody Civil War, America abolished the evil institution of slavery where a person could own another person as property. On June 4, 1919, the 19th Amendment to the US Constitution fully enfranchised women. The Civil Rights Act, 1964, fulfilled legislation originally initiated by President Ulysses S. Grant in the 1870's by striking down legal discrimination based on race in government and in public accommodations and this would lead the way toward similar initiatives in the private sector. On July 1st, 1971, the 22nd Amendment to the US Constitution lowered the voting age of citizens to eighteen thus enfranchising more citizens.

The recent attacks on our founding have highlighted America's history related to race. These one-sided and divisive accounts too often ignore or fail to properly honor and recollect the great legacy of the American national experience -- our country's valiant and successful effort to shake off the curse of slavery and to use the lessons of that struggle to guide our work toward equal rights for all citizens in the present. Viewing America as an irredeemably and systemically racist country cannot account for the extraordinary role of the great heroes of the American movement against slavery and for civil rights — a great moral endeavor that, from Abraham Lincoln to Martin Luther King, Jr., was marked by religious fellowship, good will, generosity of heart, an emphasis on our shared principles, and an inclusive vision for the future.

Critical Theory, as devised by social scientists who were inspired by Conflict Theory which, in turn, was inspired by the social theories of Karl Marx, as delineated in The Communist Manifesto, is an attempt, one that has been adapted and absorbed by large swaths of our ruling elite, to divide our society into conflicting camps. They seek to accomplish this diabolical agenda, as stated in their many published doctrines and works, as a means to serve their own immediate political gain and as a long-term social goal that seeks to transform mankind into a utopian collective one world beehive.

President George Washington warned us about this in his Farewell Address of 1796, which was publicly read on the floor of the US House of Representatives from 1899 to 1984 of forces that seek to divide us.

The unity of government which constitutes you as one people is also now dear to you. It is justly so; for it is a main pillar in the edifice of your real independence, the support of your tranquility at home, your peace abroad, of your safety, of your prosperity, of that very liberty which you so highly prize. But as it is easy to foresee that, from different causes and from different quarters, much pains will be taken, many artifices employed, to weaken in your minds the conviction of this truth; as this is the point in your political fortress against which the batteries of internal and external enemies will be most constantly and actively (though often covertly and insidiously) directed, it is of infinite moment that you should properly estimate the immense value of your national Union to your collective and individual happiness; that you should cherish a cordial and immovable attachment to it; accustoming yourselves to think and speak of it as of the palladium of your political safety and prosperity; watching for its preservation with jealous anxiety; discountenancing whatever may suggest even a suspicion that it can in any event be abandoned; and indignantly frowning upon the first dawning of every attempt to alienate any portion of our country from the rest, or to enfeeble the sacred ties which now link together the various parts.

Washington recognized our freedom of religion, culture, or what he called manners and custom and, as such, our freedom to associate with various ethnic and other forms of identity within the context of placing the interests of our nation and, as such, our national culture first. Conservative social theory contains the great paradox that defines American culture which is our desire to focus on our own individual freedom and our various chosen identification with sub-culture which we balance with national identity. We choose national identity first out of self-interest, out of our long-term goals of securing a prosperous future for ourselves and our posterity, and for many additional complex reasons. President Trump's executive order stated this goal.

Bibliography

Allen, Joe, *Reaching for the Mark of the Beast,* Singularity Weekly, September 15, 2021

Billington, James H., *Fire in the Minds of Men: Origins of the Revolutionary Faith,* Transaction Publishers, 1980

Buchanan, Patrick J., The Death of the West: How Dying populations and immigrant invasions imperil our Country and Civilization, Griffin, 2002

Cohen Phillip N., *The Family: Diversity, Inequality and Social Change,* W. W. Norton, 2018

Heilbroner, Robert L., *The Worldly Philosophers: The Lives, Times and Ideas of the Great Economic Thinkers,* Simon & Schuster, 1986

Marx, Karl, *The Communist Manifesto,* 1848

Moscowitz, Charles, *On the Jewish Question, Karl Marx, anti-Semitism and the War against the West,* City Metro Enterprises, 2013.

Moscowitz, Charles, *Was Hitler a Leftist? The Nazi Missing Link,* City Metro Enterprises 2013

Packer, George, *Last Best Hope: America in Crisis and Renewal,* Farrar, Straus and Giroux, New York, 2021

Pool, James, *Hitler and his Secret Partners: Contributions, Loot and Rewards, 1933-1945,* Pocket Books, 1997

Schwab, Klaus, Malleret, Thierry, *COVID 19: The Great Reset,* July 2020, Agentur Schweiz

Schwab, Klaus, *The Forth Industrial Revolution,* 2017, Crown Publishing

The New York Times Magazine, *The 1619 Project,* August 18, 2019

The President's Advisory 1776 Commission, *The 1776 Report,* January 2021

Trump White House, Executive Orders, Executive Order Establishing The President's Advisory 1776 Commission, issued on November 2, 2020.

Washington, George, *Washington's Farewell Address to the People of the United States,* 106th Congress, 2nd session, Senate Document No. 106-21, Washington 2000